1945

Fun Facts & Trivia

ISBN: 9798342430289

© Spotty Dog Publications 2024
All Rights Reserved

	Page
Calendar	4
People in High Office	5
British News & Events	9
Worldwide News & Events	22
Births - U.K. Personalities	41
Notable British Deaths	48
Popular Music	51
Top 5 Films	57
Sporting Winners	68
Cost of Living	71

FIRST EDITION

1945

January
M	T	W	T	F	S	S
1	2	3	4	5	6	7
8	9	10	11	12	13	14
15	16	17	18	19	20	21
22	23	24	25	26	27	28
29	30	31				

☽:6 ●:14 ☾:21 ○:28

February
M	T	W	T	F	S	S
			1	2	3	4
5	6	7	8	9	10	11
12	13	14	15	16	17	18
19	20	21	22	23	24	25
26	27	28				

☽:5 ●:12 ☾:19 ○:27

March
M	T	W	T	F	S	S
			1	2	3	4
5	6	7	8	9	10	11
12	13	14	15	16	17	18
19	20	21	22	23	24	25
26	27	28	29	30	31	

☽:7 ●:14 ☾:20 ○:28

April
M	T	W	T	F	S	S
						1
2	3	4	5	6	7	8
9	10	11	12	13	14	15
16	17	18	19	20	21	22
23	24	25	26	27	28	29
30						

☽:5 ●:12 ☾:19 ○:27

May
M	T	W	T	F	S	S
	1	2	3	4	5	6
7	8	9	10	11	12	13
14	15	16	17	18	19	20
21	22	23	24	25	26	27
28	29	30	31			

☽:5 ●:11 ☾:19 ○:27

June
M	T	W	T	F	S	S
				1	2	3
4	5	6	7	8	9	10
11	12	13	14	15	16	17
18	19	20	21	22	23	24
25	26	27	28	29	30	

☽:3 ●:10 ☾:17 ○:25

July
M	T	W	T	F	S	S
						1
2	3	4	5	6	7	8
9	10	11	12	13	14	15
16	17	18	19	20	21	22
23	24	25	26	27	28	29
30	31					

☽:2 ●:9 ☾:17 ○:25 ☽:31

August
M	T	W	T	F	S	S
		1	2	3	4	5
6	7	8	9	10	11	12
13	14	15	16	17	18	19
20	21	22	23	24	25	26
27	28	29	30	31		

●:8 ☾:16 ○:23 ☽:30

September
M	T	W	T	F	S	S
					1	2
3	4	5	6	7	8	9
10	11	12	13	14	15	16
17	18	19	20	21	22	23
24	25	26	27	28	29	30

●:6 ☾:14 ○:21 ☽:28

October
M	T	W	T	F	S	S
1	2	3	4	5	6	7
8	9	10	11	12	13	14
15	16	17	18	19	20	21
22	23	24	25	26	27	28
29	30	31				

●:6 ☾:14 ○:21 ☽:27

November
M	T	W	T	F	S	S
			1	2	3	4
5	6	7	8	9	10	11
12	13	14	15	16	17	18
19	20	21	22	23	24	25
26	27	28	29	30		

●:4 ☾:12 ○:19 ☽:26

December
M	T	W	T	F	S	S
					1	2
3	4	5	6	7	8	9
10	11	12	13	14	15	16
17	18	19	20	21	22	23
24	25	26	27	28	29	30
31						

●:4 ☾:12 ○:19 ☽:26

People in High Office

Monarch - King George VI
Reign: 11th December 1936 - 6th February 1952
Predecessor: Edward VIII
Successor: Elizabeth II

United Kingdom

Prime Minister
Winston Churchill

Conservative Party
10th May 1940 -
26th July 1945

Prime Minister
Clement Attlee

Labour Party
26th July 1945 -
26th October 1951

Ireland

Taoiseach Of Ireland
Éamon de Valera

Fianna Fáil
29th December 1937 -
18th February 1948

Canada

Prime Minister
Mackenzie King

Liberal Party
23rd October 1935 -
15th November 1948

United States

President

Franklin D. Roosevelt	**Harry S. Truman**
Democratic Party	
4th March 1933 - 12th April 1945	12th April 1945 - 20th January 1953

Australia	Prime Minister John Curtin (1941-1945) Frank Forde (1945) Ben Chifley (1945-1949)
Brazil	President Getúlio Vargas (1930-1945) José Linhares (1945-1946)
China	Premier Chiang Kai-shek (1939-1945) Soong Tse-ven (1945-1947)
Cuba	President Ramón Grau (1944-1948)
Egypt	Prime Minister Ahmad Mahir Pasha (1944-1945) Mahmoud El Nokrashy Pasha (1945-1946)
France	Chairmen of the Provisional Government Charles de Gaulle (1944-1946)
Nazi Germany	Chancellor Adolf Hitler (1933-1945) Joseph Goebbels (1945) Lutz Graf Schwerin von Krosigk (1945)
India	Viceroy of India Archibald Percival Wavell (1943-1947)

Italy	Prime Minister Ivanoe Bonomi (1944-1945) Ferruccio Parri (1945) Alcide De Gasperi (1945-1946)
Japan	Prime Minister Kuniaki Koiso (1944-1945) Kantarō Suzuki (1945) Naruhiko Higashikuni (1945) Kijūrō Shidehara (1945-1946)
Mexico	President Manuel Ávila Camacho (1940-1946)
New Zealand	Prime Minister Peter Fraser (1940-1949)
Russia	Communist Party Leader Joseph Stalin (1922-1952)
South Africa	Prime Minister Jan Smuts (1939-1948)
Spain	Prime Minister Francisco Franco (1938-1973)
Turkey	Prime Minister Şükrü Saracoğlu (1942-1946)

BRITISH NEWS & EVENTS

JAN

7th — Field Marshal Bernard Montgomery holds a press conference at Zonhoven, Belgium, describing his contribution to the Battle of the Bulge. During the conference Montgomery downplays the contribution of American generals, further souring his relationship with his American counterparts for the rest of the war.

23rd — The Industrial and Commercial Finance Corporation (ICFC) is established by the Bank of England, and major British banks, to provide long-term investment funding for small and medium-sized enterprises. *NB: The company was rebranded Investors in Industry in 1983, and later privatised as 3i in 1994.*

31st — Burma Campaign: The British 3rd Commando Brigade defeats the Imperial Japanese Army's 54th Division to bring to an end the Battle of Hill 170.

FEB

4th February: The Yalta Conference, a week-long meeting of the heads of government of the United Kingdom, United States and Soviet Union, to discuss the postwar reorganisation of Germany and Europe, is held near Yalta in the Crimea. *Photo: Prime Minister Winston Churchill, American President Franklin Roosevelt, and Soviet leader Joseph Stalin at the Yalta Conference.*

FEB

- **9th** — Black Friday: In Førde Fjord, Norway, a force of Allied Bristol Beaufighter aircraft (from 65 Squadron RAF) suffers heavy losses during an unsuccessful attack on the German destroyer Z33 and its escorting vessels.
- **13th** — A joint British and American aerial bombing attack on the city of Dresden, the capital of the German state of Saxony, begins. Over the next couple of days heavy bombers, 772 from the RAF and 527 from the USAAF, drop more than 3,900 tons of high-explosive bombs and incendiary devices on the city. The bombing results in a lethal firestorm which destroys more than 1,600 acres of the city centre and kills up to 25,000 people.
- **16th** — Over a period of four days the RAF attacks and almost entirely destroys the town of Wesel, softening up the German defences on the east bank of the river Rhine in preparation for an Allied assault into the Nazi heartland.

23rd February: The RAF carry out a raid on the southwestern German town of Pforzheim in what is one of the most devastating area bombardments of the war. Some 17,600 people are killed, 31.4% of the town's population, and 83% of the town's buildings are destroyed. *Photo: Pforzheim c. 1946.*

- **27th** — The RAF sends 435 bombers to attack Mainz, Germany. They drop 1,500 tons of bombs on large areas of the Neustadt, killing 1,209 people and destroying 80% of the city.

MAR

- **3rd** — The Royal Air Force accidentally bombs the Bezuidenhout neighbourhood in The Hague, Netherlands, killing 532 people.

MAR

4th March: Princess Elizabeth, at her own request, joins the Auxiliary Territorial Service (ATS) as a truck driver / mechanic, and starts her training in Camberley, Surrey. In an announcement from Buckingham Palace, King George VI declares that he has granted the Princess a commission with the honorary rank of second subaltern, but that she will not receive any special privileges because of her personal rank. *Photo: Princess Elizabeth explains to the Queen about the engine she has been working on, April 1945.*

10th	Seventy German prisoners of war tunnel their way out of Island Farm Camp 198 at Bridgend, South Wales, in what is the biggest escape attempt by German POWs in Britain during WWII; all the escapees are recaptured within a week.
14th	The RAF's Grand Slam bomb, the largest and most powerful conventional aerial bomb used by either side during the war, is used for the first time on the Bielefeld railway viaduct. *NB: Grand Slams were the most effective bombs used by the Allies until the advent of atomic weapons.*
16th	RAF Bomber Command orders 225 Lancasters and 11 Mosquitos to attack and bomb Würzburg as part of the Allied strategic bombing campaign against Nazi Germany. In less than 20 minutes 82% of the city is in ruins and 5,000 people have been killed.
17th	A lone Heinkel 111 bomber opens fire and drops bombs on people leaving the Savoy Cinema on Holderness Road, Kingston upon Hull. Thirteen people are killed and another 22 are injured; they are last recorded victims of the war from a manned German strike on British soil.
20th	Troops of the British 14th Army liberate Mandalay (Burma's second city) after three years of occupation by the Japanese. *NB: The success allows the 14th Army to head south towards its main objective, the Burmese capital Rangoon.*

MAR

- **22nd** — The Cathedral and the historic centre of Hildesheim, Germany, a key target of Allied Bomber Command, is destroyed by British and Canadian aircraft. Around 1,500 civilians are killed in the attack.
- **23rd** — Lt. Gen. Miles Dempsey becomes the first senior British commander to cross the Rhine during the Allied invasion of Germany.
- **23rd** — S.S. Cars Limited shareholders agree in general meeting to change the company's name to Jaguar Cars Limited. Chairman William Lyons explains "Unlike S.S. the name Jaguar is distinctive and cannot be connected or confused with any similar foreign name".
- **24th** — Operation Varsity: British and American airborne divisions, led by Field Marshal Bernard Montgomery, capture bridges across the river Rhine to aid the Allied advance. *NB: Involving more than 16,000 paratroopers and several thousand aircraft, it is the largest airborne operation ever conducted on a single day and in one location.*

25th March: Prime Minister Winston Churchill, Field Marshall Bernard Montgomery, Field Marshal Sir Alan Brooke, and U.S. General William Simpson cross the east bank of the Rhine, south of Wesel, in an American Landing Craft Vehicle Personnel (Higgins boat). *Photo: The Prime Minister and party walking ashore after crossing the Rhine.*

- **27th** — The final two V-2 rocket attacks on Britain strike Hughes Mansions in Stepney, East London, killing 134, and Kynaston Road in Orpington, Kent, killing one, Ivy Millichamp, the last civilian casualty of the war on British soil.

MAR

29th	The last enemy action of any kind on British soil occurs when a V-1 Flying Bomb strikes Datchworth in Hertfordshire. There are no fatalities or injuries.

APR

	Sybil Campbell is appointed a stipendiary magistrate in London by Home Secretary Herbert Morrison, making her the first woman in the United Kingdom to become a professional judge.
13th	Robert McIntyre wins the Motherwell by-election with a narrow majority of 617 votes over his Labour opponent, and notably becomes the first Scottish National Party candidate to be elected as a Member of Parliament. *NB: McIntyre lost the seat in the general election three months later.*
15th	Bergen-Belsen concentration camp is liberated by British and Canadian forces. On entering the camp, the troops discover over 13,000 unburied bodies and around 60,000 inmates, many of whom are suffering from typhus, dysentery and starvation. *NB: Despite massive efforts to help the survivors some 14,000 of them died after liberation.*
19th	Dr Geoffrey Fisher is enthroned as the 99th Archbishop of Canterbury.

21st April: Ivor Novello's musical "Perchance to Dream", starring Novello, Roma Beaumont and Margaret Rutherford, premieres in London at the Hippodrome Theatre. *NB: "Perchance to Dream" was one of Novello's most successful works and enjoyed an original run of 1,022 performances (the longest of any of Novello's runs) before it finally closed on 11th October 1948. Photos: Ivor Novello and Roma Beaumont in "Perchance to Dream" at the Hippodrome Theatre, c. 1945.*

25th	RAF Bomber Command carries out its last major strategic raid of the war when it sends 107 Avro Lancasters to destroy the oil refinery at Vallø (Tønsberg) in southern Norway.
26th	The British 3rd Infantry Division, under General Lashmer Whistler, captures the German port of Bremen.
29th	Operation Manna: Over a period of 10 days, 242 British Avro Lancaster bombers drop nearly 7,000 tons of food into the Netherlands to prevent the starvation of the civilian population. *NB: Operation Manna was the world's first airborne humanitarian mission.*

MAY

2nd	The British 11th Armoured Division, commanded by Major-General Philip Roberts, liberates Lübeck in Northern Germany.
2nd	Operation Dracula: Indian and British troops successfully liberate the Burmese capital Rangoon after Japanese forces evacuate the city.
3rd	As part of general strikes on shipping in the Baltic Sea, the Royal Air Force sinks three ships in the Bay of Lübeck. Unbeknown to them the ships (the SS Cap Arcona, the SS Deutschland, and the SS Thielbek) were packed with concentration-camp inmates. Around 7,000 people are killed.
4th	All German armed forces in northwest Germany, Denmark and the Netherlands, surrender unconditionally to Field Marshal Bernard Montgomery at Luneburg Heath, south of Hamburg.
7th	The SS Avondale Park is torpedoed and sunk by German submarine U-2336 off the Firth of Forth; two of the 38 crew are lost. *NB: The SS Avondale Park was the last British-flagged merchant ship lost to German action during WWII.*
7th	The unconditional surrender of the German Third Reich is signed at Supreme Headquarters Allied Expeditionary Force (SHAEF) at Reims in northeastern France. The document of surrender is signed by General Alfred Jodl on behalf of Germany and comes into effect the following day.

8th May: Eight days after the suicide of Adolf Hitler in Berlin and the collapse of Nazi rule, Victory in Europe Day is celebrated throughout the United Kingdom. Prime Minister Winston Churchill makes a victory speech welcoming the news that the war in Europe has ended, but includes a note of caution, saying "We may allow ourselves a brief period of rejoicing; but let us not forget for a moment the toil and efforts that lie ahead" (in reference to the fact that Japan was still to be defeated).

MAY

8th May: To celebrate VE Day, colourful bunting and flags line the streets of villages, towns and cities across Britain as communities come together. Events are organised to mark the occasion including parades, thanksgiving services and street parties. The Royal Family play a central role in London's victory celebrations and make numerous appearances on the balcony at Buckingham Palace throughout the day. *Photo: King George VI, Queen Elizabeth, and Princesses Elizabeth and Margaret are joined by Prime Minister Winston Churchill on the balcony of Buckingham Palace, VE Day.*

9th	German forces on both Jersey and Guernsey, the two largest Channel Islands, surrender.
23rd	Winston Churchill forms a "caretaker" Conservative Party administration pending a general election on 26th July 1945 (officially ending the wartime Coalition government).
23rd	The Flensburg Government is dissolved by the Allies and Germany's President Karl Dönitz, and its Chancellor Lutz Graf Schwerin von Krosigk, are arrested by British RAF Regiment personnel.
23rd	Heinrich Himmler, the former head of the Nazi SS and architect of Hitler's program to exterminate European Jews, commits suicide by biting into a hidden potassium cyanide pill at the headquarters of the Second British Army at Luneburg in Northern Germany.
25th	British science fiction writer Arthur C. Clark privately circulates a paper proposing relay satellites in geosynchronous orbit. Not considered seriously at the time it becomes a reality within 20 years with the launching of the first commercial geostationary communication satellite, Intelsat I (Early Bird), on 6th April 1965.
28th	American-born, Irish-raised, fascist and Nazi propaganda broadcaster William Joyce, known as "Lord Haw-Haw", is captured at Luneburg near the German border with Denmark. *Follow up: Joyce is transported to England and charged with high treason, a crime for which he is convicted on 19th September 1945. An attempted appeal fails and the 39-year-old Joyce is executed (by hanging) at Wandsworth Prison on 3rd January 1946.*

JUN

5th	The Allied Control Council, the military occupation governing body of Germany (made up of the Commanders-in-Chief of the United States, United Kingdom, the Soviet Union, and France), sign the Berlin Declaration and formally assume "supreme authority" over Germany.
7th	Peter Grimes, an opera in three acts by Benjamin Britten, premieres at Sadler's Wells Theatre in London and is hailed by the public and critics.
12th	The Council for the Encouragement of Music and the Arts, appointed in January 1940 to help promote and maintain British culture, is renamed the Arts Council of Great Britain.
15th	Parliament passes the Family Allowances Act to provide payments to families with children. *NB: The Act came into effect on 6th August 1946 and paid an allowance of five shillings per week for each child in a family other than the eldest. It was payable whilst the child was of school age (5-14 years), or up to the age of 16 if they were apprenticed or in full-time school education.*
18th	The demobilisation of the approximately five million wartime servicemembers in the British Armed Forces begins. *NB: Demobilisation and reassimilation of this vast force back into civilian life was one of the first and greatest challenges facing the postwar British government. Fun fact: Decommissioned soldiers received a demobilisation grant and a set of civilian clothing which included the so-called "demob suit", two shirts, a tie, raincoat, hat and some shoes.*
26th	The United Nations is formally established with the signing of the UN Charter by 50 nations in San Francisco. *NB: The Charter came into force on 24th October 1945 following ratification by the five permanent members of the United Nations Security Council - China, France, the Soviet Union, United Kingdom, and United States.*

JUL

5th	The first general election in the U.K. since 1935 is held. Polling in some constituencies is delayed for local holiday reasons, and the counting of votes is put off until 26th July to provide time for service personnel stationed overseas to vote.
17th	Potsdam Conference begins: The three main Allied leaders, British Prime Minister Winston Churchill, U.S. President Harry Truman, and Soviet leader Joseph Stalin, meet in Potsdam, Germany, to negotiate terms for the end of the war. *NB: During the conference, on 24th July, President Truman officially informs the Soviet leader that the United States has successfully detonated the first atomic bomb (16th July).*
21st	The Proms returns to the Royal Albert Hall for its 51st season (it was relocated temporarily to the Beford Corn Exchange in 1944 amid concerns for the hall's safety because of increased German bombing). The First Night concert includes William Walton's Memorial Fanfare for Henry Wood, as well as a performance of Elgar's Cockaigne (In London Town).
26th	The general election results are announced; the governing Conservative Party, led by Winston Churchill, is soundly defeated by Clement Attlee's Labour Party, who win 49.7% of the popular vote and a majority of 145 seats. *NB: The result means that for the very first time Labour will govern Britain with a majority in the House of Commons.*

JUL

26th July: Labour leader Clement Attlee celebrates his party's election victory with his wife Violet in Stepney, London.

29th	The BBC Light Programme radio station is launched as a replacement for the wartime BBC General Forces Programme. Concentrating on mainstream light music and entertainment, the new service broadcasts from 9.00am-midnight Monday to Friday, and 8.00am-11.00pm on Sundays.

AUG

2nd	Clement Davies replaces Sir Archibald Sinclair as leader of the Liberal Party.
5th	The Giles Family cartoon first appears in the Sunday Express. *Fun facts: Over the course of the next 45 years the Giles Family, created by cartoonist Carl Giles, would appear in over two thousand cartoons in the Sunday Express and Daily Express.*
8th	Britain, the United States, the USSR and France sign the London Agreement establishing an International Military Tribunal for the trial of Nazi war criminals.
14th	Some 300 Polish-Jewish children, liberated from Theresienstadt concentration camp, arrive at Windermere in the Lake District to recuperate before their resettlement.
14th	At the stroke of midnight Prime Minister Clement Attlee broadcasts to the nation news of Japan's unconditional surrender. Speaking from 10 Downing Street, Attlee expresses his gratitude to Britain's allies, in particular the United States "without whose prodigious efforts the war in the East would still have many years to run".

AUG

15th August: Victory over Japan Day, marking the surrender of Japanese forces to the Allies (and effectively the end of the Second World War), is celebrated across the United Kingdom and by Allied countries around the globe. Two days of national holiday are announced and thousands of people around country take to the streets to celebrate. In London huge crowds gather in Trafalgar Square, Piccadilly Circus and outside Buckingham Palace. *Photo: Crowds at Piccadilly Circus celebrate VJ Day.*

17th	George Orwell's political allegory Animal Farm is published by Secker and Warburg. *Fun facts: Animal Farm was very well-received by the public and sold more than 500,000 copies in its first year. As of 2023, it has sold over eleven million copies.*
30th	British sovereignty of Hong Kong is restored after the Imperial Japanese Army hands the territory over to the Royal Navy. The 30th August is declared as "Liberation Day" and becomes a public holiday in Hong Kong (until 1997). *NB: General Takashi Sakai, who led the invasion of Hong Kong and served as governor-general during the Japanese occupation, was tried as a war criminal, convicted, and executed on the 30th September 1946.*

SEP

2nd	The official Japanese Instrument of Surrender is signed by representatives from the Empire of Japan and Allied nations in a ceremony on board the American battleship USS Missouri in Tokyo Bay. American General of the Army Douglas MacArthur, the Commander in the Southwest Pacific and Supreme Commander for the Allied Powers, accepts the surrender on behalf of the Allies. Allied signatories to the Instrument of Surrender includes representatives from the United States, China, United Kingdom (Admiral Sir Bruce Fraser), Soviet Union, Australia, Canada, France, Netherlands, and New Zealand.

SEP

2nd September: Japanese Foreign Minister Mamoru Shigemitsu signing the Instrument of Surrender on behalf of the Japanese Government, formally ending World War II.

2nd	Lend-Lease from the United States terminates. *NB: Lend-Lease was a policy under which the United States supplied the United Kingdom (and other Allied nations) with food, oil, and materiel between 1941 and 1945. The aid was given free of charge on the basis that such help was essential for the defence of the United States.*
12th	The Japanese Army formally surrenders to the British in Singapore marking the end of Japanese occupation in Southeast Asia.
28th	Piccadilly Circus tube station becomes the first to be lit by fluorescent tube lighting.
30th	A sleeper train from Perth to London Euston derails at Bourne End, Hertfordshire, killing 43 people and injuring another 64.

OCT

1st	Operation Backfire: The first of three (possibly four) V-2 rockets are launched near Cuxhaven, within the British Occupation zone in Germany, in order to demonstrate the weapon to Allied personnel.
15th	The Fifth Pan-African Congress opens at the Chorlton-on-Medlock Town Hall in Manchester.
27th	Battle of Surabaya: Indonesian soldiers and militia fight British and British Indian troops in Surabaya as a part of the Indonesian National Revolution against the re-imposition of Dutch colonial rule.
27th	The Philharmonia Orchestra, founded by Walter Legge, plays its first concert in London.

NOV

14th	Future Conservative Prime Minister Harold Macmillan, who lost his Stockton seat in the July 1945 landslide Labour general election victory, is returned to Parliament after winning a by-election in Bromley, Kent.
15th	Prime Minister Clement Attlee, American President Harry Truman, and Canadian Prime Minister Mackenzie King, issue a communiqué proposing the establishment of a commission, under the United Nations, that would investigate ways of eliminating the destructive use of atomic energy while promoting its "widest use for industrial and humanitarian purposes". *Follow up: The proposal led to the foundation of the United Nations Atomic Energy Commission (UNAEC) on 24th January 1946 (the very first resolution of the United Nations General Assembly).*
15th	Gainsborough Pictures releases the period melodrama "The Wicked Lady" starring Margaret Lockwood, James Mason and Patricia Roc. *Fun fact: "The Wicked Lady" was the most popular film at the British box office in 1946.*
16th	The United Nations Educational, Scientific and Cultural Organization (UNESCO), largely developed by the U.K. Minister of Education Rab Butler, is founded at a United Nations Conference in London.

17th November: Wing Commander Hugh Joseph Wilson, Commandant of the Empire Test Pilots' School at RAF Cranfield, sets a new world air speed record for a jet fighter of 606.4 mph *(975.9 km/h)* at Herne Bay in Kent. Photo: *Hugh Wilson's Gloster Meteor F Mk.4 Britannia (EE454) takes off on its way to breaking the world air speed record.*

26th	David Lean's romantic tragedy film "Brief Encounter", based on Noël Coward's one-act play Still Life (1936) and starring Celia Johnson and Trevor Howard, is released to cinema audiences. *Fun facts: "Brief Encounter" received three nominations at the 19th Academy Awards in 1947, Best Director, Best Actress and Best Adapted Screenplay. In 1999, the British Film Institute ranked it as the second-greatest British film of all time.*
28th	British fascist and Nazi collaborator John Amery pleads guilty to treason and is sentenced to hang Wandsworth Prison on 19th December 1945.

DEC

10th Scottish physician and microbiologist Alexander Fleming, German-born British biochemist Ernst Chain, and Australian pharmacologist and pathologist Howard Florey, share the Nobel Prize in Physiology or Medicine "for the discovery of penicillin and its curative effect in various infectious diseases".

30th December: The cargo ship Tilapa docks in Avonmouth, Bristol, loaded with a consignment of 10 million bananas from Kingston, Jamaica. Hundreds of children, most of whom had never seen a banana before, were there to greet it. As the ship docked a crew member threw a banana on to the quayside where it was caught by the 10-year-old daughter of a dock worker. It was the first banana to reach Britain since 1940.
Photo: 12-year-old Daphne Philips gleefully eats one of the first bananas to arrive in Britain after the war, given to her by Alderman James Owen JP, Lord Mayor of Bristol.

Worldwide News & Events

1. 1st January: Germany begins Operation Bodenplatte, an attempt by the Luftwaffe to cripple Allied air forces in the Low Countries. Although the operation results in almost 500 Allied airplanes being destroyed, it fails to achieve air superiority. *NB: Bodenplatte was the last large-scale strategic offensive operation mounted by the Luftwaffe during World War II.*
2. 1st January: Chenogne massacre: Near the village of Chenogne, Belgium, around 80 German prisoners are killed by American forces of the 11th Armored Division.

3. 6th January: Whilst on leave from the Navy future president of the United States, Lieutenant George H. W. Bush, marries future First Lady, Barbara Pierce, in Rye, New York. *Fun facts: The couple went on to have 6 children and were married for 73 years. Photo: George and Barbara Bush on their wedding day.*

4. 6th January: The Warner Bros. anthropomorphic striped skunk, Pepe Le Pew, makes his debut in the Looney Tunes cartoon "Odor-able Kitty".
5. 9th January: 175,000 troops from the U.S. Sixth Army launch an assault at Lingayen Gulf on the largest Philippine Island of Luzon (occupied by Japan since 1942). *Follow up: The Allies took control of all the strategic and economically important locations on Luzon by early March. Pockets of Japanese soldiers did hold out in the mountains after this but most ceased resistance with Japan's unconditional surrender in August 1945 (a few though did hold out for many years afterwards). The Battle of Luzon saw 217,000 Japanese combatants killed and 9,050 taken prisoner, 8,310 Americans killed and 29,560 wounded, and over 150,000 Filipinos killed (overwhelmingly civilians who were murdered by Japanese forces).*
6. 12th January: The Soviet Union begins the Vistula-Oder Offensive against the German Army in Eastern Europe.

7. 16th January: In Berlin, Adolf Hitler takes up residence in the Führerbunker with his long-term partner, Eva Braun, and various staff members.
8. 17th January: The First Polish Army and the Soviet Red Army enter Warsaw and, after encountering weak resistance from German troops, "liberate" the Polish capital.
9. 19th January: Soviet forces liberate the Lodz Ghetto (established by the German authorities for Polish Jews and Roma following the Invasion of Poland) and find just 877 Jews left alive. *NB: Of the 223,000 Jews in Lodz before the German invasion only 10,000 actually survived the Holocaust.*
10. 20th January: Franklin D. Roosevelt is inaugurated to an unprecedented fourth term as President of the United States. Missouri Senator Harry S. Truman is sworn in as Vice President. *Fun fact: Roosevelt remains the only American president to have served for more than two terms.*
11. 21st January: German Admiral Karl Dönitz orders the start of Operation Hannibal, the mass evacuation by sea of German troops and civilians from the Courland Pocket, East Prussia, and the Polish Corridor, due to the threat from the advancing Soviet Red Army. *NB: Over a period of 15 weeks, Operation Hannibal saw an estimated 800,000 - 900,000 German civilians, and 350,000 soldiers, transported across the Baltic Sea to Germany and occupied Denmark.*
12. 23rd January: Representatives of the provisional government of Hungary sign an armistice with the Allies in Moscow.

13. 26th January: At Holtzwihr in north-eastern France, 19-year-old U.S. Army Staff Sergeant Audie Murphy single-handedly holds off a company of German soldiers for an hour, killing or wounding 50 of them. Although he sustains a leg wound during his stand, he only stops after running out of ammunition. Murphy then rejoins his men and, disregarding his own injury, leads them back to repel the Germans in a successful counterattack. For his actions at Holtzwihr, Murphy is awarded the Medal of Honor, the U.S. Armed Forces' highest military decoration. *NB: Widely celebrated as the most decorated American combat soldier of World War II, Murphy received every military combat award for valour available from the U.S. Army. Additionally,*  *he was also awarded the French Legion of Honor and Belgian Croix de guerre for his heroism. Photo: U.S. Army publicity photo of soldier and actor Audie Murphy, circa 1948.*

14. 27th January: Soviet soldiers liberate Auschwitz-Birkenau, a complex of over 40 concentration and extermination camps operated by Nazi Germany in occupied Poland. *NB: Approximately 1.1 million men, women and children were murdered at Auschwitz-Birkenau (over 90% of them Jewish).*

15. 30th January: The MV Wilhelm Gustloff, carrying over 10,000 mainly German civilians during Operation Hannibal, is hit by three torpedoes from the Soviet submarine S-13 in the Baltic Sea. The ship sinks less than an hour later with the loss of over 9,000 men, women and children. It is worst recorded maritime disaster in history. *Photo: The MV Wilhelm Gustloff, pre-WWII.*

16. 30th January: On what is the twelfth anniversary of the Nazis coming to power, Adolf Hitler makes his last ever public speech. Broadcast over the radio, Hitler appeals to the German people to keep up a spirit of resistance.
17. 30th January: Raid at Cabanatuan: U.S. Army Rangers, Alamo Scouts, and Filipino guerrillas, liberate 489 POWs and 33 civilians from the Japanese-held camp near Cabanatuan, Nueva Ecija, Philippines.
18. 31st January: American soldier Eddie Slovik is executed by firing squad for desertion - he is the first U.S. soldier since the American Civil War, and last to date, to be executed for this offence. *NB: Although over 21,000 American soldiers were given varying sentences for desertion during World War II, including 49 death sentences, Slovik's death sentence was the only one that was carried out.*
19. 3rd February: Battle of Manila: U.S. forces enter the outskirts of Manila, the capital city of the Philippines, and begin a month-long battle to capture it from the Japanese Imperial Army. The battle results in the deaths of at least 100,000 civilians and the complete devastation of the city. *NB: The Battle of Manila is widely considered to be one of the most intense and worst urban battles ever fought by American forces.*
20. 3rd February: "The Three Caballeros", Walt Disney Productions' seventh feature film, is released. *Fun fact: "The Three Caballeros" was one of the first feature-length films to incorporate traditional animation with live-action actors.*
21. 10th February: The German transport ship SS General von Steuben is sunk by the Soviet submarine S-13 while evacuating German military personnel, wounded soldiers, and civilian refugees during Operation Hannibal. An estimated 4,000 people are killed.
22. 12th February: In the United States a devastating tornado outbreak across Mississippi and Alabama kills 45 people and injures 427 others.
23. 13th February: German and Hungarian forces surrender Budapest after a 50-day-long encirclement of the city by Soviet and Romanian forces.

24. 15th February: Raymond L. Libby of American Cyanamid's research laboratories at Stamford, Connecticut, announces that he has discovered a method to make penicillin pills to replace injection by needle.
25. 15th February: Venezuela and Uruguay declare war on Germany and Japan.
26. 16th February: American ground forces of the 503rd PRCT land on Corregidor Island in the Philippines. The recapture of the island takes 10 days; 6,600 Japanese and 207 American troops are killed in the battle.

27. 19th February: Battle of Iwo Jima: United States Marines land on Iwo Jima tasked with capturing the island and its two airfields. The subsequent five-week battle sees some of the fiercest and bloodiest fighting of the Pacific War. By the time the island is captured on 26th March some 6,821 American and 18,000 Japanese troops have been killed. *NB: The Medal of Honor was awarded to 27 recipients (14 posthumously) for their actions during the Battle of Iwo Jima. Photo: Joe Rosenthal's Pulitzer Prize winning picture showing six U.S. Marines raising the American flag at the top of Mount Suribachi, Iwo Jima, 23rd February 1945.*

28. 21st February: Italian campaign: The Battle of Monte Castello ends when Brazilian troops expel German forces from a pivot point in the North Apennines (on the border between the regions of Tuscany and Emilia-Romagna) where their artillery had been impeding the advance of the Eighth British Army toward Bologna.
29. 23rd February: Turkey declares war on Germany and Japan.
30. 23rd February: The Nazi German garrison in Poznan, Poland, capitulates to Red Army and Polish troops after a month-long battle.
31. 24th February: Prime Minister Ahmad Mahir Pasha of Egypt is assassinated in the Egyptian parliament immediately after declaring war on Germany and Japan.
32. 24th February: In Bucharest, Romania, the Communist Party and its allies organise a mass rally in front of the Royal Palace to call for Prime Minister Nicolae Radescu's resignation. During the protest several people are killed by communist agents after they open fire from the Interior Ministry building across the street, a diversion which allows the Soviets to accuse Radescu of having ordered the army to fire.

33.	28th February: Andrey Vishinsky, the Soviet vice commissioner of foreign affairs and president of the Allied Control Commission for Romania, travels to Bucharest to compel Nicolae Radescu to resign as premier. Radescu resigns his position the next day.
34.	2nd March: The rocket-propelled Bachem Ba 349 Natter makes its first manned vertical take-off flight at Stetten am kalten Markt, in Baden-Württemberg, Germany. The launch fails and the pilot, Lothar Sieber, dies. *NB: The Natter was the first manned rocket developed as an anti-aircraft weapon.*
35.	3rd March: Finland declares war on Germany, retroactive to 19th September 1944 following terms of 1944 Moscow Armistice.
36.	3rd March: Pawłokoma massacre: A Polish Home Army unit massacres between 150 and 500 Ukrainian civilians in the village of Pawłokoma in south-eastern Poland.
37.	4th March: The Swiss cities of Basel and Zürich are accidentally bombed by American B-24 Liberators - their intended target had been Freiburg in Germany; 5 people are killed.
38.	6th March: A Communist-led government is formed in Romania under Petru Groza following the forced resignation of Nicolae Radescu.
39.	6th March: Dutch resistance fighters ambush and attempt to execute SS general Hanns Albin Rauter, the SS and Police Leader in the occupied Netherlands. In a reprisal organised by SS-Brigadeführer Karl Eberhard Schöngarth, the Germans execute 117 political prisoners at the location of the attack, 50 prisoners in Kamp Amersfoort, and 40 prisoners each in The Hague and Rotterdam.
40.	7th March: American troops capture Ludendorff Bridge over the river Rhine at Remagen, Germany. Over the next 10 days six Allied divisions are able to cross the damaged bridge before it collapses.
41.	7th March: In Belgrade, communist revolutionary and politician Josip Broz Tito forms the Provisional Government of the Democratic Federal Yugoslavia after King Peter II agrees to a power transition.
42.	9th - 10th March: Bombing of Tokyo: 279 USAAF B-29 Superfortress heavy bombers conduct a devastating firebombing raid on Tokyo. In what is the single most destructive conventional air attack of the war, over 90,000 Japanese people are killed, mostly civilians, and one million are left homeless; the Americans lose 14 aircraft and 96 airmen in the attack.
43.	10th March: Field Marshal Albert Kesselring succeeds Gerd von Rundstedt as Germany's Commander-in-Chief West following Rundstedt's disastrous loss of the intact Ludendorff Bridge during the Battle of Remagen.
44.	11th March: The Empire of Japan establishes the Empire of Vietnam, a puppet state with Vietnamese Emperor Bao Dại as its ruler.
45.	12th March: Swinemünde is destroyed by 671 American bombers who unleash 1609 tons of bombs on the city. Estimates put the number killed at between 8,000 and 23,000.
46.	12th March: New York becomes the first American state to enact legislation prohibiting discrimination in employment based on race, colour, creed and national origin.
47.	15th March: The 17th Academy Awards ceremony, honouring the best films of 1944, is held at Grauman's Chinese Theater in Hollywood, California. Hosted by John Cromwell and Bob Hope, the winners include Leo McCarey's "Going My Way" (Best Picture), Bing Crosby (Best Actor), and Ingrid Bergman (Best Actress).
48.	16th - 17th March: 331 American B-29 bombers launch a firebombing attack against the city of Kobe, Japan. The resulting firestorm destroys an area of three-square miles and kills 8,841 of the city's residents.

49. 18th March: 1,221 USAAF bombers leave England and set a course for Berlin, Germany, to attack rail stations and tank factories in support of the Russian advance. The bombers drop 3,000 tons of explosives in what is the largest raid on Berlin of the war. More than half of the bombers, 714 planes, sustain damage from German anti-aircraft fire, and 24 bombers and 6 fighters are lost on the mission; 178 Americans are killed, wounded or captured. Although it is impossible to know the exact number of Germans killed in the raid, conservative estimates put German losses around 3,000 civilians.
50. 18th March: Battle of Kolberg: Soviet and Polish forces take the Baltic seaport of Kolberg (one of the key German positions in the Pomeranian Wall) from Nazi forces.
51. 18th March: Montreal Canadien's Maurice "Rocket" Richard becomes the first player in National Hockey League history to score 50 goals in one season.

52. 19th March: Off the coast of Japan, a single Yokosuka D4Y "Judy" dive bomber hits the American aircraft carrier USS Franklin with two semi-armour-piercing bombs, crippling the ship. At the time she is struck, Franklin has 31 armed and fuelled aircraft warming up on her flight deck, and these planes catch fire almost immediately; 724 men are killed and 265 wounded. *NB: The Franklin suffered the most severe damage and highest casualties experienced by any U.S. fleet carrier that survived World War II. Photo: The USS Franklin, afire and listing, after being hit during the Japanese air attack (photographed from the cruiser USS Santa Fe which was assisting with firefighting and rescue work).*

53. 19th March: Adolf Hitler issues the "Nero Decree" ordering that all industries, military installations, machine shops, and transportation and communications facilities in Germany be destroyed ahead of Allied advances. Reich Minister of Armaments and War Production, Albert Speer, who is placed in charge of its implementation, deliberately disobeys the order.

54. 22nd March: Following adoption of the Alexandria Protocol in 1944, the Arab League is founded in Cairo, Egypt. *NB: The Arab League aimed to be a regional organisation of Arab states with a focus on developing economy's, resolving disputes and coordinating political aims - it has received a relatively low level of cooperation throughout its history.*
55. 24th March: Billboard publishes its first popular albums chart in the U.S. and lists the King Cole Trio's self-titled debut record (released by Capitol) as its first No.1.

MODEL SHEET

56. 24th March: The cartoon character Sylvester the Cat debuts in the Warner Bros. animated short "Life with Feathers" directed by Friz Freleng. *Fun facts: Sylvester appeared in 103 cartoons in the golden age of American animation, lagging only behind superstars Bugs Bunny, Porky Pig, and Daffy Duck. Three of his cartoons have won Academy Awards, the most for any Looney Tunes character.*

57. 27th March: Argentina declares war on Germany and Japan.
58. 29th March: Film star James Stewart is promoted to full colonel, one of the few Americans to rise from private to colonel in just four years. *Fun facts: On 23rd July 1959, Stewart was promoted to brigadier general and became the highest-ranking actor in American military history. In total Stewart served for 27 years, officially retiring from the U.S. Air Force on 31st May 1968.*
59. 31st March: Tennessee Williams' memory play "The Glass Menagerie" premieres at the Playhouse Theatre on Broadway. *NB: "The Glass Menagerie" was Williams' first successful play; he went on to become one of America's most highly regarded playwrights.*
60. 1st April: Battle of Okinawa: The Tenth U.S. Army lands on the island of Okinawa, Japan, in the largest amphibious assault in the Pacific Theater of WWII. The 82-day battle lasts until 22nd June 1945, and is the bloodiest and fiercest of the Pacific War. At least 90% of the buildings on the island are destroyed and 242,046 people are killed including; 149,634 Okinawans, 77,823 Imperial Japanese soldiers, and 14,010 Americans.
61. 4th April: The U.S. 4th Armored Division, led by Brigadier General Joseph F. H. Cutrona, liberates the Ohrdruf concentration camp in Germany. It is the first Nazi concentration camp liberated by the Americans.
62. 6th April: Sarajevo, Bosnia, is liberated from Nazi Germany and the Independent State of Croatia (a fascist puppet state) by Yugoslav Partisans.

63. 6th April: On Bougainville Island, the Battle of Slater's Knoll concludes with a decisive victory for the Australian Army's 7th Brigade.
64. 7th April: The Japanese battleship Yamato (the largest battleship in the world) and nine escorts are attacked by American carrier-borne aircraft in the East China Sea. The Yamato and five of the escorts are sunk with the loss of 4,137 lives.
65. 7th April: After the resignation of Kuniaki Koiso, 77-year-old Kantaro Suzuki becomes the new Prime Minister of Japan.
66. 7th April: The only flight the Sonderkommando Elbe, a Luftwaffe task force assigned to bring down heavy bombers by ramming them in mid-air, takes place over Germany. The force of 120 Messerschmitt Bf 109s manage to ram 15 U.S. Eighth Air Force bombers, downing eight of them. *NB: The German pilots were expected to parachute out either just before or after they had collided with their target.*
67. 8th April: The film adaptation of Betty Smith's novel "A Tree Grows in Brooklyn" premieres in the United Kingdom. Directed Elia Kazan (his first feature film) the picture wins Oscars for both James Dunn (Best Supporting Actor) and Peggy Ann Garner (Academy Juvenile Award) at the 18th Academy Awards. *NB: In 2010, "A Tree Grows in Brooklyn" was selected for preservation in the U.S. National Film Registry by the Library of Congress.*
68. 9th April: Soviet forces of the 1st Baltic Front and the 3rd Belorussian Front capture the city of Königsberg (present day Kaliningrad, Russia) from the Germans after four days of urban warfare.
69. 9th April: Abwehr conspirators Wilhelm Canaris, Hans Oster, Hans von Dohnanyi, and pastor Dietrich Bonhoeffer, who all worked with the German resistance against the Nazi regime, are hanged at Flossenberg concentration camp for high treason.
70. 9th April: Johann Georg Elser, who carried out an elaborate assassination attempt on Adolf Hitler and other high-ranking Nazi leaders in Munich in November 1939, is executed at Dachau concentration camp.
71. 9th April: American National Football League Commissioner Elmer Layden decrees that all players must wear long stockings because of their "unsightly legs". *Fun fact: Frank Gore of the San Francisco 49ers was issued a $10,500 fine in 2013 after wearing his socks far too low for the NFL's liking.*
72. 11th April: American troops liberate the Buchenwald Nazi concentration camp freeing over 21,000 prisoners. *NB: One of those prisoners was Eliezer Wiesel who went on to win the Nobel Peace Prize in 1986.*
73. 12th April: President Roosevelt dies suddenly at Warm Springs, Georgia, of an intracerebral hemorrhage; Vice President Harry S. Truman is sworn in as the 33rd President of the United States later that evening at the White House.
74. 12th April: A tornado outbreak occurs across the Midwestern United States causing $7.63 million in damage; 128 people are killed and 1,001 are injured.
75. 13th April: Gardelegen massacre: Under the direction of the SS, 1016 slave labourers, who were part of a transport train evacuated from the Mittelbau-Dora and Hannover-Stöcken concentration camps, are killed after being forced into a large barn and set on fire.
76. 14th April: SS leader Heinrich Himmler orders the commandants of the Dachau and Flossenbürg concentration camps to immediately evacuate all prisoners, informing them that "Not a single prisoner must fall alive into enemy hands".
77. 14th April: Razing of Friesoythe: The 4th Canadian (Armoured) Division deliberately destroys the German town of Friesoythe, on the orders of Major General Christopher Vokes, in retaliation for the killing of the battalion's commander, Lieutenant-Colonel Frederick Wigle.
78. 15th April: Soviet forces capture the city of Vienna, Austria, after a month long offensive.

79.	16th April: The Battle of Berlin begins, opening with two Soviet fronts attacking the city from the east and south, while a third overruns German forces positioned to the north.
80.	16th April: The MV Goya, a Norwegian motor freighter used as a troop transport ship by Nazi Germany, is sunk by the Soviet submarine L-3 in the Baltic Sea while evacuating German military and civilian personnel during Operation Hannibal. Out of the roughly 6,700 passengers and crew onboard there are just 183 survivors.
81.	19th April: Rodgers and Hammerstein's second musical "Carousel", adapted from Ferenc Molnar's 1909 play Liliom, opens at the Majestic Theatre on Broadway. The musical is immediate hit with both critics and audiences. *Fun fact: In 1999, Time magazine named Carousel the best musical of the 20th century.*
82.	20th April: After a fierce four-day battle U.S. Army troops capture the German city of Nuremberg, previously the site of the Nuremberg rallies.

83. 20th April: On his 56th birthday, Adolf Hitler leaves his Führerbunker to award Iron Crosses to boy soldiers of the Hitler Youth at the Reich Chancellery in Berlin. It will be his last trip to the surface from the underground bunker. *NB: Later that afternoon Berlin is bombarded by Soviet artillery for the first time. Photo: Hitler awarding medals to Hitler Youth members in the garden of the Reich Chancellery.*

84.	22nd April: At a meeting in the Führerbunker, after learning that SS-Obergruppenführer Felix Steiner has been unable to launch a counterattack on the Soviet forces which have completely surrounded Berlin, Adolf Hitler flies into a rage, denounces the German Army, and finally concedes that "everything is lost".
85.	22nd April: Heinrich Himmler, through the President of the Swedish Red Cross Count Folke Bernadotte, puts forth an offer to the Supreme Commander of the Allied Forces, Dwight D. Eisenhower, of a German surrender to the Western Allies, but not the Soviet Union. The message takes 48 hours to reach the Allies who do not take it seriously. *Follow up: When word of Himmler's offer reached Hitler on the night of 28th April, he declared him a traitor, stripped him of all titles and ranks, and ordered his arrest.*
86.	23rd April: The U.S. 90th Infantry Division liberates the main Flossenbürg Nazi concentration camp.

87. 23rd April: Hermann Göring sends the Göring Telegram to Hitler, seeking confirmation that he should take over the leadership of Germany in accordance with the decree of 29th June 1941. *Follow up: Two days later Hitler issues a telegram to Göring telling him that he has committed "high treason" and gives him the option of resigning all of his offices "for reasons of health", in exchange for his life. Göring subsequently resigns.*
88. 24th April: Retreating German troops destroy all the bridges over the Adige River in Verona, Italy, including the historic Ponte di Castelvecchio and Ponte Pietra.
89. 25th April: Elbe Day: American and Soviet troops link up at the Elbe River, near Torgau, effectively cutting Germany in two.

90. 27th April: With the last German formations having withdrawn from Finland to Norway, the Lapland War, and thus World War II in Finland, comes to an end. *Photo: Finnish soldiers raise the war flag at the three-country cairn between Norway, Sweden, and Finland, to mark the end of World War II in Finland.*

91. 27th April: The provisional government of Austria, headed by Karl Renner, asserts its independence from Germany.
92. 29th April: The bodies of Benito Mussolini, his mistress Clara Petacci, and other fascist supporters, are hung by their heels at an Esso petrol station in the Piazzale Loreto, Milan, following their execution by Italian partisans the previous day.
93. 29th April: At the Royal Palace of Caserta in Italy, representatives of the German command and Italian fascist regime sign an unconditional instrument of surrender for all German and Italian forces in Italy (effective on 2nd May).
94. 29th April: Prisoners of Dachau concentration camp are liberated by soldiers of the U.S. Army's 42nd Infantry Division. *NB: Dachau was the first concentration camp to be constructed by the Nazis and had imprisoned over 180,000 individuals by the time it was liberated. The estimated number of people murdered at the camp is believed to be around 41,500.*

95.	29th April: Adolf Hitler marries his longtime mistress Eva Braun in a closed civil ceremony in the Führerbunker, and signs his last will and testament.
96.	29th April: U.S. combat medic and conscientious objector, Private Desmond Doss, saves 75 wounded soldiers in the Battle of Okinawa. *NB: For this, and other actions, he is awarded the Medal of Honor. Fun fact: Doss's experiences were the subject of the Oscar-winning film Hacksaw Ridge (2016).*
97.	30th April: Adolf Hitler and his wife of one day, Eva Braun, commit suicide in the Führerbunker in Berlin, Hitler via a gunshot to the head and Braun by biting into a cyanide capsule.
98.	30th April: Hitler is succeeded by Admiral Karl Dönitz as President of Germany and Joseph Goebbels as Chancellor.
99.	1st May: Joseph Goebbels carries out his sole official act as Chancellor of Germany, dictating a letter to the Soviet commander in Berlin advising of Hitler's death and requesting a ceasefire. When the latter is refused, he and his wife Magda kill their six children and commit suicide themselves.
100.	1st May: Hundreds of people kill themselves in the town of Demmin, Pomerania, after three days of Soviet soldiers looting and destroying the town, committing rapes, and carrying out executions. Estimates put the number of people committing suicide at between 700 and 1,200.
101.	2nd May: Battle of Berlin: The Soviet army captures the German capital and forces its commander, General Helmuth Weidling, to surrender.

102. 2nd May: Rocket scientist Wernher von Braun, and several members of his team, surrender to a private from the U.S. 44th Infantry Division in Ruette, Bavaria. *Follow up: On 20th June U.S. Secretary of State, Edward Stettinius Jr., approves the transfer of von Braun and his specialists to the United States. A Nazi Party and Allgemeine-SS member, von Braun later becomes one of the most important rocket developers and champions of space exploration in the twentieth century. NB: Von Braun was the director of NASA's Marshall Space Flight Center and the chief architect of the Saturn V launch vehicle, the super booster that propelled Americans to the Moon. Photo: Werner von Braun (with his arm in a cast) and other members of the German V-2 rocket development team shortly after their surrender to U.S. forces.*

103.	5th May: The American 11th Armored Division liberates the prisoners of Mauthausen concentration camp, the main camp of a group with nearly 100 further subcamps located throughout Austria and southern Germany. Overall, more than 90,000 of the 190,000 people deported to Mauthausen died there or in one of its subcamps. *NB: Mauthausen was the last Nazi concentration camp to be liberated by the Allies.*
104.	5th May: A Japanese Fu-Go balloon bomb kills five children and a grown woman, Elsie Mitchell, near Bly, Oregon, when it explodes shortly after being found in Fremont National Forest. *NB: They are the only people killed by an enemy attack on the American mainland during World War II.*
105.	5th May: The cartoon character Yosemite Sam debuts in the Warner Bros. animated short "Hare Trigger" directed by Friz Freleng.
106.	6th May: American broadcaster Mildred Gillars (aka "Axis Sally") delivers her last propaganda broadcast to Allied troops. *Follow up: After her capture in Berlin on 15th March 1946, Gillars became the first woman to be convicted of treason against the United States and was sentenced to ten to thirty years' imprisonment in March 1949. She was eventually paroled on 10th June 1961.*
107.	7th May: At 02:41 Central European Time, General Alfred Jodl signs the unconditional German Instrument of Surrender ending Germany's participation in World War II.
108.	7th May: The Pulitzer Prize for a Novel awarded to John Hersey for "A Bell for Adano".
109.	8th May: Setif and Guelma massacre: In response to shots being fired during at a protest in Setif, Algeria, native Algerians riot in the town, and others attack French settlers in the surrounding countryside resulting in 102 deaths. The French colonial authorities and European settlers retaliate by killing between 6,000 and 45,000 Muslims in the region.
110.	8th May: Nazi Field Marshal Hermann Goering surrenders to the U.S. Seventh Army in Bavaria.
111.	14th May: At the University of California Hospital in San Francisco, physician Joseph G. Hamilton injects misdiagnosed cancer patient Albert Stevens (CAL-1) with 131 kBq (3.55 µCi) of plutonium without his knowledge. Stevens lives another 20 years, surviving the highest known accumulated radiation dose in any human.
112.	15th May: Retreating troops from the former puppet Independent State of Croatia (intermingled with fleeing civilians) attempt to surrender to the British Army at Bleiburg. The British refuse to accept their surrender and direct them to surrender to Yugoslav Partisans, which they do. A number of refugees try to escape and the Yugoslav's open fire on them killing several dozen people. The remainder, on the orders of Yugoslavia's Prime Minister Josip Tito, are force-marched through Croatia and Serbia and interned or massacred; the number of people killed on marches and in labour camps is estimated to be in the hundreds of thousands.
113.	7th June: King Haakon VII of Norway and the rest of the Norwegian royal family return to Norway aboard the cruiser HMS Norfolk. They arrive back in Oslo to cheering crowds exactly five years to the day after leaving for exile in Britain.
114.	11th June: William Lyon Mackenzie King is re-elected for a third term as the Prime Minister of Canada. Although his Liberal Party falls short of a majority, it is able to rule as a majority government with the support of Independent Liberal MPs.
115.	12th June: The Yugoslav Army departs Trieste leaving the New Zealand Army in control.
116.	19th June: In Chile, 355 men succumb to carbon monoxide poisoning after smoke from a nearby fire traps them in tunnels at the El Teniente mine. Another 747 men are injured due to smoke inhalation.

117. 22nd June: The Battle of Okinawa: The U.S. Tenth Army hold a flag-raising ceremony to mark the end of organised resistance on Okinawa. Rather than surrender many of the remaining Japanese forces choose to sacrifice themselves in the name of the emperor; they also force civilians to kill themselves to avoid being taken prisoner. *NB: Okinawa remained under U.S. occupation until 24th November 1971, and to this day there is still a significant American force garrisoned on the island.*

118. 24th June: Soviet Armed Forces hold a victory parade in Moscow's Red Square to celebrate the defeat of Nazi Germany. Ordered by Joseph Stalin, it is the longest and largest military parade ever held in the Soviet capital, and involves some 40,000 Red Army soldiers and 1,850 military vehicles. *Photo: Officers of the 2nd Belorussian Front marching in the victory parade in Red Square.*

119. 25th June: Fianna Fáil politician Sean T. O'Kelly is elected as the second President of Ireland.
120. 5th July: Australian Prime Minister John Curtin dies in office from heart failure at the age of 60. His deputy, Frank Forde, replaces him in a caretaker capacity until a Labor Party leadership election can be held. *Follow up: Forde is replaced by Ben Chifley on 13th July 1945, making him the shortest-serving prime minister in Australia's history.*
121. 6th - 7th July: Schio massacre: Former Italian partisans of the Garibaldi Brigade and officers of the Auxiliary Partisan Police open fire on prisoners in the city jail of Schio in northern Italy; 54 inmates are killed, 14 of them women.
122. 14th July: Italy declares war on Japan.
123. 15th July: The first Scott Morrison Award of Minor Hockey Excellence is given; its first recipient is future Hockey Hall of Famer Gordie Howe.
124. 16th July: The U.S. Army detonates the world's first atomic bomb in the Jornada del Muerto desert, about 35 miles southeast of Socorro, New Mexico. Code named "Trinity", the bomb, part of the Manhattan Project, unleashes an explosion equivalent to that of 25 kilotons of TNT.

125. 23rd July: French World War I hero Marshal Philippe Pétain goes on trial in a packed Paris courtroom. He is charged with treason, for surrendering to the Nazis in the summer of 1940 and then collaborating with them as head of the Vichy regime. *Follow up: Pétain was convicted in August 1945 and sentenced to death. His sentence was immediately commuted to life imprisonment by the President of the Provisional Government of the French Republic, Charles De Gaulle.*

126. 28th July: A fog blind B-25 Mitchell bomber flown by Lieutenant Colonel William F. Smith, a veteran of more than 1,000 combat flying hours, crashes into the 79th floor of the Empire State Building in New York; 14 people are killed (including all three aboard the plane), and 24 injured. *Guiness World Record: Amazingly 20-year-old "Elevator girl" Betty Lou Oliver survives falling 75 stories (around 300m) after elevator support cables snap and send her hurtling down to the building's basement. As of 2024, this remains the longest fall survived in an elevator. Photos: The Empire State Building shortly after the crash / Betty Lou Oliver surprises her husband by showing him she can walk again.*

127. 30th July: The American heavy cruiser USS Indianapolis is hit by torpedoes from the Imperial Japanese Navy submarine I-58 and sinks within 12 minutes in the Philippine Sea. Of 1,195 crewmen aboard, approximately 300 go down with the ship. The remaining 890 face exposure, dehydration, saltwater poisoning, and shark attacks while stranded in the open ocean. After 3½ days the survivors are spotted by the crew of a PV-1 Ventura on a routine patrol flight. By the time they are rescued there are only 316 men left alive. *NB: On 20th December 2018, the crew of Indianapolis was collectively awarded a Congressional Gold Medal.*

128. 31st July: Pierre Laval, the fugitive former leader of Vichy France, surrenders to Allied soldiers in Austria. *Follow up: Laval was extradited to France where he was convicted of treason and executed by firing squad on 15th October 1945.*

129. 6th August: The USAAF Boeing B-29 Superfortress "Enola Gay", piloted by Colonel Paul W. Tibbets Jr. and co-piloted by Captain Robert A. Lewis, drops a uranium-235 atomic bomb, codenamed "Little Boy", on the Japanese city of Hiroshima. The bomb explodes with a blast yield equivalent to 15 kilotons of TNT and results in the deaths of between 70,000 and 140,000 people.

130. 8th August: The Soviet Union declares war on Japan.

131. 9th August: The USAAF B-29 Superfortress "Bockscar", piloted by Major Charles W. Sweeney and co-piloted by First Lieutenant Charles Donald Albury, drops a plutonium-239 atomic bomb, codenamed "Fat Man", on the Japanese city of Nagasaki. The bomb explodes with a blast yield equivalent to 21 kilotons of TNT and results in the deaths of between 40,000 and 70,000 people.
132. 9th August: The Soviet Union begins its army offensive against Japan in the Japanese-held Chinese region of Manchuria.

133. 14th August: Emperor Hirohito announces that he has accepted the terms of the Potsdam Declaration. In the United States, President Truman breaks the news of the unconditional surrender of Japan to reporters gathered at the White House, and huge street parties break out across the country. *Photo: The iconic photo of a sailor kissing a nurse in Times Square, New York, to celebrate the long awaited-victory over Japan.*

134. 15th August: A riot involving thousands of drunken people, the vast majority of them Navy enlistees, breaks out in San Francisco while the city is celebrating Japan's surrender. Confined mostly to downtown San Francisco, the riot (the deadliest in the city's history) sees 6 women raped, 1,000 people injured, and 11 killed.
135. 16th August: Puyi, the last Chinese Emperor and ruler of Manchukuo, is captured en-route to Japan by Soviet troops.
136. 17th August: President of the Philippines, José P. Laurel, issues an executive proclamation putting an end to the Second Philippine Republic.
137. 17th August: Sukarno and Mohammad Hatta declare Indonesia (Dutch East Indies) independent from the Netherlands.
138. 18th August: The Indian nationalist leader Subhas Chandra Bose is killed after the bomber in which he is being transported crashes upon take off from Japanese-ruled Formosa (now Taiwan).

139.	19th August: Following Japan's surrender the August Revolution, a revolt against French and Japanese colonial occupation of Vietnam, begins with the Viet Minh seizing control of Hanoi.
140.	21st August: Manhattan Project physicist Harry Daghlian accidentally drops a tungsten carbide brick onto a plutonium-gallium alloy bomb core, exposing himself to a lethal dose of neutron radiation and becoming the first known fatality due to a criticality accident 25 days later.
141.	25th August: In response to the August Revolution, Bao Dai abdicates as Emperor of Vietnam, ending 2,000 years of dynastic and monarchic rule in the country and 143 years of the Nguyen dynasty.
142.	31st August: The formation of the Liberal Party of Australia is formally announced at the Town Hall in Sydney. *NB: After an initial loss to Labor at the 1946 election, the Liberal Party, led by Robert Menzies, came to power in coalition with the Country Party at the 1949 election, and stayed in office for a record 23 years.*
143.	2nd September: Foreign Minister Mamoru Shigemitsu and Army General Yoshijiro Umezu sign the Japanese Instrument of Surrender on behalf of the Emperor of Japan, the Japanese Government, and the Japanese Imperial General Headquarters, formally bringing World War II to an end.
144.	2nd September: Communist revolutionary Ho Chi Minh, leader of the Viet Minh Front, declares independence and proclaims the creation of the Democratic Republic of Vietnam (North Vietnam). *NB: Vietnamese independence wasn't officially recognised until 1954.*
145.	5th September: 26-year-old code clerk Igor Gouzenko walks out of the Russian embassy in Ottawa, Canada, carrying a briefcase with numerous documents implicating the Soviet Union in spy rings in both the United States and Canada.
146.	8th September: American troops land at Incheon in the southern half of the Korean Peninsula, effectively ending Japan's 35-year rule of Korea. Shortly afterwards they establish the United States Army Military Government in Korea (USAMGIK). *NB: With U.S. troops occupying the south of Korea and the Soviet Union the north, they temporarily agreed to divide the country at the 38th parallel in order to oversee the removal of Japanese forces. This arrangement proved to be the indirect beginning of a divided Korea, and led to the Korean War (1950-1953).*
147.	9th September: The Chairman of the Nationalist Government of China, Chiang Kai-shek, officially accepts Japan's surrender in the China Theatre, at Nanking.
148.	10th September: Norwegian Nazi leader Vidkun Quisling is found guilty of charges including embezzlement, murder, and high treason against the Norwegian state, and is sentenced to death. *Follow up: On 24th October 1945, Quisling, protesting his innocence to the last, was executed by firing squad at Akershus Fortress in Oslo.*
149.	10th September: Mike the Headless Chicken, a five-and-a-half-month-old male Wyandotte chicken, is decapitated by farmer Lloyd Olsen of Fruita, Colorado. Mike survives for another 18 months and achieves national fame until his death in March 1947. *NB: Mike holds the Guinness World Records record for the longest surviving chicken without a head.*
150.	11th September: Hideki Tojo, the Prime Minister of Japan during most of World War II, attempts to commit suicide by shooting himself in the chest to avoid facing an Allied war crimes tribunal. The shot misses his heart and he survives. *Follow up: Tojo was tried by the International Military Tribunal for the Far East for war crimes and found guilty on 12th November 1948. Sentenced to death, he was executed by hanging 41 days later on 23rd December 1948.*
151.	11th September: In the Netherlands, physician Willem J. Kolff performs the first successful kidney dialysis using his artificial kidney machine.

152.	17th September: Typhoon Ida makes landfall near Makurazaki on the Japanese mainland. The storm, one of the deadliest in Japanese history, kills more than 2,000 people, many in the Hiroshima Prefecture.
153.	18th September: Hundreds of white students at Froebel School in Gary, Indiana, walk out of their classes to protest against the integration of African American students at the institution.
154.	23rd September: The first Cavalcade of Jazz outdoor concert is held at Wrigley Field in Los Angeles, California. Produced by African American entrepreneur Leon Hefflin Sr., and attended by some 15,000 people, the stars at the concert include, amongst others, Count Basie, The Honey Drippers, Valaida Snow, Joe Turner, The Peters Sisters, and Slim and Bam.
155.	23rd September: World heavyweight boxing champion Joe Louis is awarded the Legion of Merit. Receipt of the honour qualifies him for immediate release from the U.S. Army (1st October 1945).
156.	3rd October: The World Federation of Trade Unions is founded by the World Trade Union Congress in Paris.
157.	3rd October: In his first-ever live performance (broadcast over WELO Radio) Elvis Presley sings "Old Shep" in a youth talent contest at the Mississippi-Alabama Fair and Dairy Show, held in Tupelo, Mississippi. Dressed up as a cowboy, and standing on a chair so that he can reach the microphone, the 10-year-old future King of Rock and Roll wins fifth prize - $5.00 in fairground ride tickets.
158.	5th October: The motion picture "The Lost Weekend", starring Ray Milland and Jane Wyman, is released in the United Kingdom. *NB: "The Lost Weekend" was nominated for seven Oscars and won four at the 18th Academy Awards: Best Picture, Best Director, Best Actor, and Best Adapted Screenplay.*
159.	5th October: Hollywood Black Friday: A six-month strike by set decorators, represented by the Conference of Studio Unions (CSU), boils over into a bloody riot at the gates of Warner Bros.' studios in Burbank, California.
160.	8th October: American defence contractor Raytheon files a patent for the microwave oven. Developed by inventor Percy Spencer, the patent is granted on 24th January 1950. *Fun facts: The first commercial microwave oven was called Radarange and was marketed in 1947. It cost $5,000, weighed about 340kg, and stood 6 feet tall / Percy Spencer was inducted into the Inventors Hall of Fame in 1999.*
161.	10th October: The Nazi Party is formally abolished by the Allied Control Council.
162.	16th October: The Food and Agriculture Organization, a specialised agency of the United Nations to lead international efforts to defeat hunger and improve nutrition and food security, is established at a meeting in Quebec City, Canada.
163.	17th October: Loyalty Day (Argentina): A mass labour demonstration is held at the Plaza de Mayo, in downtown Buenos Aires, to demand the release of Juan Peron. It is considered the foundational moment of the Peronist movement.
164.	18th October: The President of Venezuela, Isaias Medina Angarita, is overthrown by a coalition of military forces and the political party Accion Democratica. Romulo Betancourt is named as provisional president of Venezuela.
165.	29th October: Getulio Vargas is deposed as the President of Brazil by the Brazilian Army; Jose Linhares is named as the country's interim president.
166.	29th October: Anna M. Rosenberg becomes the first American citizen to receive the Medal of Freedom. She received the honour for her development of the "Buffalo Plan", which solved many wartime defence manufacturing problems. *NB: The Medal of Freedom was established by President Truman to honour civilians whose actions had "aided in the war efforts of the United States and its allies during and beyond World War II".*

167. 11th November: Two new elements, americium and curium, are announced by Glenn T. Seaborg after a question by a child contestant on an American live national radio show called Quiz Kids. *NB: The elements, discovered by Seaborg, Leon O. Morgan, Ralph A. James, and Albert Ghiorso, at the University of California, Berkeley, were actually supposed to be officially unveiled on 16th November during a national meeting of the American Chemical Society. Fun facts: Between 1944 and 1958, Seaborg identified eight elements - americium (95), curium (96), berkelium (97), californium (98), einsteinium (99), fermium (100), mendelevium (101), and nobelium (102). Photo: Dr. Glenn T. Seaborg with the periodic table of elements he revised, circa 1951.*

168.	11th November: Marshal Josip Broz Tito and the People's Front win a decisive majority (90%) in the Yugoslavian parliamentary election (due to an opposition boycott, the governing People's Front was the only organisation to participate in the elections). *NB: Eighteen days after the elections, the newly elected legislature formally abolished the monarchy and declared the Federal People's Republic of Yugoslavia.*
169.	16th November: The cartoon character Casper the Friendly Ghost, created by Seymour Reit and Joe Oriolo, debuts in the Noveltoon "The Friendly Ghost".
170.	20th November: The first of a series of trials against representatives of defeated Nazi Germany, for plotting and carrying out invasions of other countries across Europe and atrocities against their citizens in World War II, begins at the Palace of Justice in Nuremberg, Germany.
171.	21st November: The United Auto Workers (UAW) union organise 320,000 hourly workers to form a nationwide strike against Detroit-based General Motors. *Follow up: The strike ended after 113 days, on 13th March 1946, with workers receiving a raise of 17.5% (they wanted 30%), paid vacations and overtime.*
172.	28th November: An earthquake strikes Balochistan in British India with a moment magnitude of 8.1 and a maximum Mercalli intensity of X (Extreme). The quake, and a tsunami caused by the quake along the Makran coastal region, results in as many as 4,000 people being killed.

173.	2nd December: The de Gaulle Government enacts a law to nationalise all major French deposit banks.
174.	5th December: Flight 19: A group of five TBM Avenger torpedo bombers disappear over the Bermuda Triangle after losing contact during a U.S. Navy training exercise from Naval Air Station Fort Lauderdale in Florida. A Martin PBM Mariner flying boat is launched to search for Flight 19 but that also disappears. *NB: To date no trace of the missing aircraft, or the 27 aviators, has been ever been found.*
175.	9th December: American General George S. Patton is injured in an automobile accident when the driver of his limousine, PFC Horace Woodring, crashes into the side of an Army truck in Manheim, Germany. Patton, who is paralysed in the accident, is rushed to hospital in Heidelberg, but dies from his injuries 12 days later.
176.	10th December: The Nobel Peace Prize is awarded to the former U.S. Secretary of State Cordell Hull "for his indefatigable work for international understanding and his pivotal role in establishing the United Nations".
177.	10th December: Chilean poet Gabriela Mistral becomes the first Latin American to be awarded the Nobel Prize for Literature "for her lyric poetry which, inspired by powerful emotions, has made her name a symbol of the idealistic aspirations of the entire Latin American world".
178.	27th December: The International Monetary Fund, based on the ideas of senior U.S. Treasury department official Harry Dexter White and British economist and philosopher John Maynard Keynes, is formally established.

BIRTHS

British Personalities

BORN IN 1945

Barry John
b. 6th January 1945
d. 4th February 2024

Rugby union fly-half who won 25 caps for Wales and 5 for the British Lions.

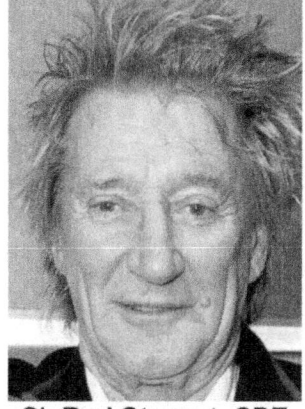

Sir **Rod Stewart**, CBE
b. 10th January 1945

Singer and songwriter who is one of the best-selling music artists of all time.

Princess Michael of Kent
b. 15th January 1945

Member of the British royal family who has written several books on European royalty.

Eric Stewart
b. 20th January 1945

Singer-songwriter, multi-instrumentalist and record producer (The Mindbenders, 10cc).

Martin Shaw
b. 21st January 1945

Stage, television and film actor.

Marti Caine
b. 26th January 1945
d. 4th November 1995

Comedienne, actress, dancer, presenter, singer and writer.

Roy Chubby Brown
b. 3rd February 1945

Comedian, writer and actor.

Gerald Davies, CBE, DL
b. 7th February 1945

Rugby union wing who won 46 caps for Wales and 5 for the British Lions.

Elkie Brooks
b. 25th February 1945

Rock, blues and jazz singer.

Eric Clapton, CBE
b. 30th March 1945

Rock and blues guitarist, singer and songwriter.

Johnnie Walker, MBE
b. 30th March 1945

Radio disc jockey and broadcaster.

Sir **Martyn Lewis**, CBE
b. 7th April 1945

Television news presenter and broadcast journalist.

Ritchie Blackmore
b. 14th April 1945

Guitarist and founding member of rock bands Deep Purple and Rainbow.

Alan Ball, MBE
b. 12th May 1945
d. 25th April 2007

Footballer who was the youngest player in England's 1966 World Cup winning squad.

Pete Townshend
b. 19th May 1945

Co-founder, guitarist and principal songwriter of the rock band the Who.

Derek Underwood, MBE
b. 8th June 1945
d. 15th April 2024

Cricketer who played in 86 Tests and 26 One Day Internationals for England.

Pat Jennings, CBE
b. 12th June 1945

Goalkeeper who played 119 matches for Northern Ireland over a period of 22 years.

Nicola Pagett
b. 15th June 1945
d. 3rd March 2021

Actress whose career spanned 35 years.

Ken Livingstone
b. 17th June 1945

Politician who has served as a Labour MP and the Mayor of London (2000-2008).

Colin Blunstone
b. 24th June 1945

Singer and songwriter who first found fame as the lead singer of the Zombies.

Ken Buchanan, MBE
b. 28th June 1945
d. 1st April 2023

Boxer who in 1971 briefly reigned as the undisputed World Lightweight Champion.

John Motson, OBE
b. 10th July 1945
d. 23rd February 2023

Football commentator.

Virginia Wade, OBE
b. 10th July 1945

Former World No.2 tennis player who won three major singles championships.

John Lowe, MBE
b. 21st July 1945

Former World No.1 darts player who won the World Darts Championship three times.

Dame **Helen Mirren**, DBE
b. 26th July 1945

Multi-award-winning actress with a career spanning 60 years.

Laila Morse
b. 1st August 1945

Actress best known for her role as Mo Harris on Eastenders.

Ian Gillan
b. 19th August 1945

Singer best known for being the lead singer and lyricist for the rock band Deep Purple.

Sir **Van Morrison**, OBE
b. 31st August 1945

Singer, songwriter and musician whose recording career spans seven decades.

Martin Tyler
b. 14th September 1945

Football commentator.

Bryan Ferry, CBE
b. 26th September 1945

Singer, songwriter and frontman of the rock band Roxy Music.

Brian Connolly
b. 5th October 1945
d. 9th February 1997
Singer, songwriter, musician, actor and the lead singer of the glam rock band Sweet.

Lesley Joseph
b. 14th October 1945

Actress and broadcaster whose career on stage and screen spans over fifty years.

Hugh Fraser
b. 23rd October 1945

Actor, theatre director and author.

Bobby Knutt
b. 25th November 1945
d. 25th September 2017
Actor and comedian.

John McVie
b. 26th November 1945

Bass guitarist best known as a member of the rock band Fleetwood Mac.

Clive Russell
b. 7th December 1945

Actor.

Bobby George
b. 16th December 1945

Darts player and television presenter.

Dame **Jacqueline Wilson**, DBE, FRSL
b. 17th December 1945

Novelist known for her popular children's literature.

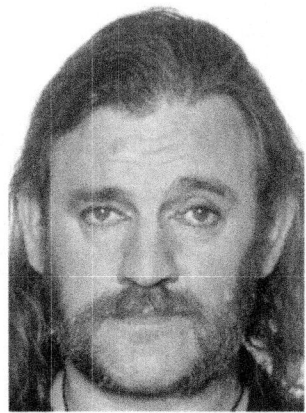

Lemmy Kilmister
b. 24th December 1945
d. 28th December 2015

Founder, lead singer, bassist and primary songwriter of the rock band Motörhead.

Davy Jones
b. 30th December 1945
d. 29th February 2012

Actor and singer best known as a member of the pop rock band the Monkees.

Notable British Deaths

2nd Jan	Admiral Sir Bertram Home Ramsay, KCB, KBE, MVO (b. 20th January 1883) - Royal Navy officer who was responsible for the Dunkirk evacuation in 1940, and planning and commanding the naval forces in the invasion of France in 1944.
6th Jan	Lieutenant-General Herbert William Lumsden, CB, DSO & Bar, MC (b. 8th April 1897) - British Army officer who fought in both the First and Second World Wars. Killed in action during a Japanese kamikaze attack whilst aboard the battleship USS New Mexico, Lumsden was the most senior British Army combat casualty of World War II.
9th Jan	Dennis O'Neill (b. 3rd March 1932) - 12-year-old Welsh boy whose death at the hands of his foster parents led to an inquiry into and overhaul of fostering provisions in Great Britain.
21st Jan	General Sir Archibald James Murray, GCB, GCMG, CVO, DSO (b. 23rd April 1860) - British Army officer who served in both the Second Boer War and the First World War.
22nd Jan	Arthur William Symons (b. 28th February 1865) - Poet, critic, translator and magazine editor.
30th Jan	Admiral Sir William Edmund Goodenough, GCB, MVO (b. 2nd June 1867) - Royal Navy officer during World War I who became the First and Principal Naval Aide-de-camp to George V (1929-1930), and in retirement served as president of the Royal Geographical Society (1930-1933).
31st Jan	Leslie Adams (b. 14th November 1909) - Rugby league footballer, also known by the nickname "Juicy", who was capped three times for England and once for Great Britain.
13th Feb	George Brown Studd (b. 20th October 1859) - Cricketer who played in four Test matches for England and later worked as a missionary Southern Los Angeles, California.

21st February: Eric Henry Liddell (b. 16th January 1902) - Scottish sprinter, rugby player and Christian missionary in China.

At the 1924 Summer Olympics in Paris Liddell won gold in the 400m - during the games he refused to run in the heats for his favoured 100 metres because they were held on a Sunday. *Fun fact: Liddell's Olympic training and racing, and the religious convictions that influenced him, are depicted in the Oscar-winning film Chariots of Fire (1981). Photo: Liddell pictured at the 1924 Olympic Games in Paris.*

5th Mar	Albert Richards (b. 19th December 1919) - World War II paratrooper and war artist.
7th Mar	Squadron Leader Daniel Trevor Bulmer "Danny" Everett, DFC and 2 Bars (b. 15th October 1920) - RAF Bomber Command / Pathfinder Force pilot and bombing leader who was decorated three times for gallantry before being killed in action.

8th Mar	Frederick Bligh Bond (b. 30th June 1864) - Architect, illustrator, archaeologist and psychical researcher.
13th Mar	Herbert Bedford (b. 23rd January 1867) - Composer, author, miniature painter and inventor.
18th Mar	William Charles Frederick Grover-Williams (b. 16th January 1903) - Grand Prix motor racing driver best known for winning the very first Monaco Grand Prix. During World War II Grover-Williams was recruited by the Special Operations Executive to work behind enemy lines in France. He was captured and imprisoned by the German Sicherheitsdienst in August 1943, and later moved to Sachsenhausen concentration camp where he was executed.
20th Mar	Lord Alfred Bruce "Bosie" Douglas (b. 22nd October 1870) - Poet and journalist best known for being Oscar Wilde's lover.
23rd Mar	Sir William Napier Shaw, FRS (b. 4th March 1854) - Meteorologist who served as president of the International Meteorological Committee (1911) and the Royal Meteorological Society (1918-1919).
23rd Mar	Steve Donoghue (b. 8th November 1884) - Flat-race jockey who won ten consecutive jockeys' championships between 1914 and 1923. As well as being a Champion Jockey, Donoghue also rode the horses Pommern and Gay Crusader to the English Triple Crown in 1915 and 1917, and was a six-time winner of the Epsom Derby.

26th March: David Lloyd George, 1st Earl Lloyd-George of Dwyfor, OM, KStJ, PC (b. 17th January 1863) - Liberal Party politician who served as the Prime Minister of the United Kingdom between 1916 and 1922.

Born in Chorlton-on-Medlock, Manchester, to Welsh parents, Lloyd George was known for leading the United Kingdom during the First World War, for social-reform policies, for his role in the Paris Peace Conference, and for negotiating the establishment of the Irish Free State. *Photo: Lloyd George, circa 1910-1915.*

29th Mar	Jack Charles Stanmore Agazarian (b. 27th August 1915) - Special Operations Executive agent in France during World War II. Agazarian was captured and imprisoned by the Germans in July 1943, and later moved to Flossenbürg concentration camp where he was executed.
7th Apr	Elizabeth, Princess Bibesco (b. Elizabeth Charlotte Lucy Asquith; 26th February 1897) - Socialite, actress and writer. Elizabeth was the daughter of former Prime Minister H. H. Asquith and the writer Margot Asquith, and the wife of Romanian prince and diplomat Antoine Bibesco.
11th Apr	Cecil Redvers Griffiths (b. 18th February 1900) - Welsh athlete who won a 4×400m relay gold medal at the 1920 Summer Olympics in Antwerp, Belgium.
18th Apr	Sir John Ambrose Fleming, FRS (b. 29th November 1849) - Electrical engineer and physicist who invented the first thermionic vacuum tube, and designed the radio transmitter with which the first transatlantic radio transmission was made.
21st Apr	Major John William Poston MC & Bar (b. 1919) - Cavalry officer best known for serving as the Aide-de-camp to Field Marshal Sir Bernard Montgomery.
3rd May	Herbert "Bertie" Farjeon (b. 5th March 1887) - Major figure in British theatre who was a presenter of revues in London's West End, a critic, lyricist, librettist, playwright, theatre manager and researcher.

15th May	Frederick Joseph Ricketts (b. 21st February 1881) - Army bandmaster and composer of marches (under the pseudonym Kenneth J. Alford) whose best-known work is the "Colonel Bogey March".
15th May	Charles Walter Stansby Williams (b. 20th September 1886) - Poet, novelist, playwright, theologian and literary critic.
27th July	Alfred James Dobbs (b. 18th June 1882) - Labour Party politician and trade unionist who died in a car accident the day after he had been elected as the MP for Smethwick.
18th Sep	Cecil Henry Middleton (b. 22nd February 1886) - Gardener and writer who was one of the earliest radio and television broadcasters on gardening for the BBC. Middleton broadcast in Britain during the 1930s and 40s, especially in relation to the "Dig for Victory" campaign during the Second World War.
21st Oct	Lionel Walker Birch Martin (b. 15th March 1878) - Businessman who co-founded the company that became Aston Martin.
31st Oct	Henry Hinchliffe Ainley (b. 21st August 1879) - Stage and film actor who served as the President of the Royal Academy of Dramatic Arts (1931-1933).
31st Oct	Alfred Edward Taylor (b. 22nd December 1869) - Idealist philosopher.
7th Nov	Alfred Ernest Dipper (b. 9th November 1885) - Cricketer who played for Gloucestershire County Cricket Club (1908-1932), and in one Test match for England (1921).
20th Nov	Francis William Aston, FRS (b. 1st September 1877) - Chemist and physicist who won the 1922 Nobel Prize in Chemistry "for his discovery, by means of his mass spectrograph, of isotopes in many non-radioactive elements and for his enunciation of the whole number rule".
21st Nov	James Quinn (b. 8th July 1878) - Footballer who played for Celtic for 15 years and became one of the club's all-time leading goal scorers. Quinn was also capped 11 times for Scotland, scoring 7 goals.
4th Dec	Arthur George Morrison (b. 1st November 1863) - Writer and journalist known for his stories about working-class life in the East End of London, and for detective stories featuring detective Martin Hewitt. He also collected Japanese art and published several works on the subject.
5th Dec	William Cosmo Gordon Lang, 1st Baron Lang of Lambeth, GCVO, GCStJ, PC (b. 31st October 1864) - Anglican prelate who served as Archbishop of York (1908-1928) and Archbishop of Canterbury (1928-1942).
14th Dec	Maud Carnegie, Countess of Southesk (b. Lady Maud Alexandra Victoria Georgina Bertha Duff; 3rd April 1893) - Granddaughter of Edward VII.
26th Dec	Admiral of the Fleet, Roger John Brownlow Keyes, 1st Baron Keyes, GCB, KCVO, CMG, DSO (b. 4th October 1872) - Naval officer with a career spanning over 50 years. Keyes also served as the MP for Portsmouth North (1934-1943).
26th Dec	Charles George Trigg (b. 5th January 1881) - Flat racing jockey who won several renowned races during his career, most notably The Oaks in 1910.

POPULAR MUSIC

Les Brown & Doris Day	No.1	Sentimental Journey
The Andrews Sisters	No.2	Rum & Coca-Cola
Perry Como	No.3	Till the End of Time
Johnny Mercer	No.4	On the Atchison, Topeka & the Santa Fe
Harry James & Kitty Kallen	No.5	It's Been a Long, Long Time
Dorothy Squires	No.6	The Gypsy
Bing Crosby & The Andrews Sisters	No.7	Don't Fence Me In
Vaughn Monroe	No.8	There! I've Said It Again
Johnny Mercer	No.9	Ac-cent-tchu-ate the Positive
Sammy Kaye	No.10	Chickery Chick

NB: During this era music was dominated by a number of Big Bands and songs could be attributed to the band leader, the band name, the lead singer, or a combination of these. On top of this the success of a song was tied to the sales of sheet music, so a popular song would often be perfomed by many different combinations of singers and bands and the contemporary charts would list the song without clarifying whose version was the major hit. With this in mind although the above chart has been compiled with best intent it does remain subjective.

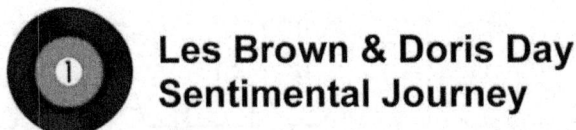
Les Brown & Doris Day
Sentimental Journey

Label:	Written by:	Length:
Columbia	Brown / Homer / Green	3 mins 8 secs

The popular song "Sentimental Journey" featured **Lester Raymond Brown** (b. 14th March 1912 - d. 4th January 2001), a jazz musician who led the big band Les Brown and His Band of Renown for over six decades (1938-2000), and **Doris Day** (b. Doris Mary Ann Kappelhoff; 3rd April 1922 - d. 13th May 2019), an actress, singer and animal rights activist who made more than 650 recordings and became one of the most popular singers of the 20th century. "Sentimental Journey" was Doris Day's first hit recording.

The Andrews Sisters
Rum & Coca-Cola

Label:	Written by:	Length:
Brunswick	Sullivan / Baron / Amsterdam	3 mins 7 secs

The Andrews Sisters were a close harmony singing group from the eras of swing and boogie-woogie. The group consisted of three sisters: LaVerne Sophia (b. 6th July 1911 - d. 8th May 1967), Maxene Angelyn (b. 3rd January 1916 - d. 21st October 1995) and Patricia Marie (b. 16th February 1918 - d. 30th January 2013). Throughout their long career the sisters sold well over 75 million records.

Perry Como
Till the End of Time

Label:	Written by:	Length:
His Master's Voice	Kaye / Mossman	3 mins 11 secs

Perry Como (b. Pierino Ronald Como; 18th May 1912 - d. 12th May 2001) was a singer and television personality. During a career spanning more than half a century he recorded exclusively for RCA Victor after signing with the label in 1943. "Mr. C.", as he was nicknamed, sold millions of records for RCA and had 2 No.1 and 14 Top 10 hits in the U.K. He received a Kennedy Center Honor in 1987 and was inducted into the Academy of Television Arts & Sciences Hall of Fame in 1990. He also has the distinction of having three stars on the Hollywood Walk of Fame for his work in radio, television and music.

Johnny Mercer
On the Atchison, Topeka & the Santa Fe

Label:	Written by:	Length:
Capitol Records	Warren / Mercer.	3 mins 6 secs

John Herndon "Johnny" Mercer (b. 18th November 1909 - d. 25th June 1976) was a lyricist, songwriter and singer, and the founder of Capitol Records. From the mid-1930s through to the mid-1950s, many of the songs Mercer wrote and performed were among the most popular hits of the time. Mercer received nineteen Academy Award nominations throughout his career, winning four Best Original Song Oscars; the first of these was "On the Atchison, Topeka & the Santa Fe" which was used in the film The Harvey Girls (1946).

 ## Harry James & Kitty Kallen
It's Been a Long, Long Time

Label:	Written by:	Length:
Columbia	Styne / Cahn	3 mins 24 secs

The hit recording "It's Been a Long, Long Time" featured **Harry Haag James** (b. 15th March 1916 - d. 5th July 1983), a musician best known as the trumpet-playing band leader of Harry James and his Orchestra, and **Kitty Kallen** (b. 25th May 1921 - d. 7th January 2016), a singer whose career spanned from the 1930s to the 1960s. "It's Been a Long, Long Time" was also notably a hit in 1945 for the iconic crooner Bing Crosby with Les Paul and His Trio.

 ## Dorothy Squires
The Gypsy

Label:	Written by:	Length:
Parlophone	Billy Reid	2 mins 51 secs

Dorothy Squires (b. Edna May Squires; 25th March 1915 - 14th April 1998) was a Welsh singer who began performing professionally aged 16 at Pontyberem working men's club in Carmarthenshire, Wales. In 1938 Squires joined the orchestra of Billy Reid, with whom she established a close personal as well as professional relationship. Reid wrote many songs for her over the years including their first big hit in 1945, "The Gypsy".

 **Bing Crosby & The Andrews Sisters**
Don't Fence Me In

Label:	Written by:	Length:
Decca	Porter / Fletcher	3 mins 1 sec

"Don't Fence Me In" was a popular song written in 1934 by Cole Porter and Robert Fletcher. It became a hit in 1944-45 for **Bing Crosby** (b. 3rd May 1903 - d. 14th October 1977) and **The Andrews Sisters**, with Vic Schoen and his Orchestra, selling more than a million copies and topping the U.S. Billboard charts for eight weeks. Other notable releases of "Don't Fence Me In" at this time were sung by Roy Rogers, Frank Sinatra and Kate Smith.

 **Vaughn Monroe**
There! I've Said It Again

Label:	Written by:	Length:
Victor	Evans / Mann	3 mins 5 secs

Vaughn Wilton Monroe (b. 7th October 1911 - d. 21st May 1973) was a baritone singer, trumpeter, big band leader and actor whose popularity was at its height in the 1940s and 1950s. Monroe formed his first orchestra in 1940, and became its principal vocalist. He has two stars on the Hollywood Walk of Fame, one for recording and one for radio.

9. Johnny Mercer
Ac-cent-tchu-ate the Positive

Label:	Written by:	Length:
Capitol	Mercer / Arlen	2 mins 39 secs

"Ac-Cent-Tchu-Ate the Positive", recorded by **Johnny Mercer** with The Pied Pipers and Paul Weston's orchestra, was written by Harold Arlen and Mercer himself. The song was nominated for the Academy Award for Best Original Song at the 18th Academy Awards after being used in the film Here Come the Waves (1944).

10. Sammy Kaye
Chickery Chick

Label:	Written by:	Length:
Victor	Lippman / Dee	2 mins 18 secs

Sammy Kaye (b. Samuel Zarnocay Jr.; 13th March 1910 - d. 2nd June 1987) was a bandleader and songwriter whose tag line, Swing and Sway with Sammy Kaye, became one of the most famous of the Big Band Era. The novelty song "Chickery Chick" was written by Sylvia Dee and Sidney Lipman, and was sung by Nancy Norman, Billy Williams and The Kaye Choir. Kaye was posthumously inducted into the Big Band and Jazz Hall of Fame in 1992.

1945: TOP FILMS

1. **The Lost Weekend** - *Paramount*
2. **The Bells of St. Mary's** - *RKO Pictures*
3. **Mildred Pierce** - *Warner Bros.*
4. **Spellbound** - *United Artists*
5. **Anchors Aweigh** - *Metro-Goldwyn-Mayer*

OSCARS

Best Picture: The Lost Weekend
Most Nominations: The Bells of St. Mary's (8)
Most Wins: The Lost Weekend (4)

Joan Crawford (Best Actress) / Ray Milland (Best Actor).

Best Director: Billy Wilder - *The Lost Weekend*

Best Actor: Ray Milland - *The Lost Weekend*
Best Actress: Joan Crawford - *Mildred Pierce*
Best Supporting Actor: James Dunn - *A Tree Grows in Brooklyn*
Best Supporting Actress: Anne Revere - *National Velvet*

The 18th Academy Awards, honouring the best in film for 1945, were presented on 7th March 1946 at Grauman's Chinese Theatre in Hollywood, California.

THE LOST WEEKEND

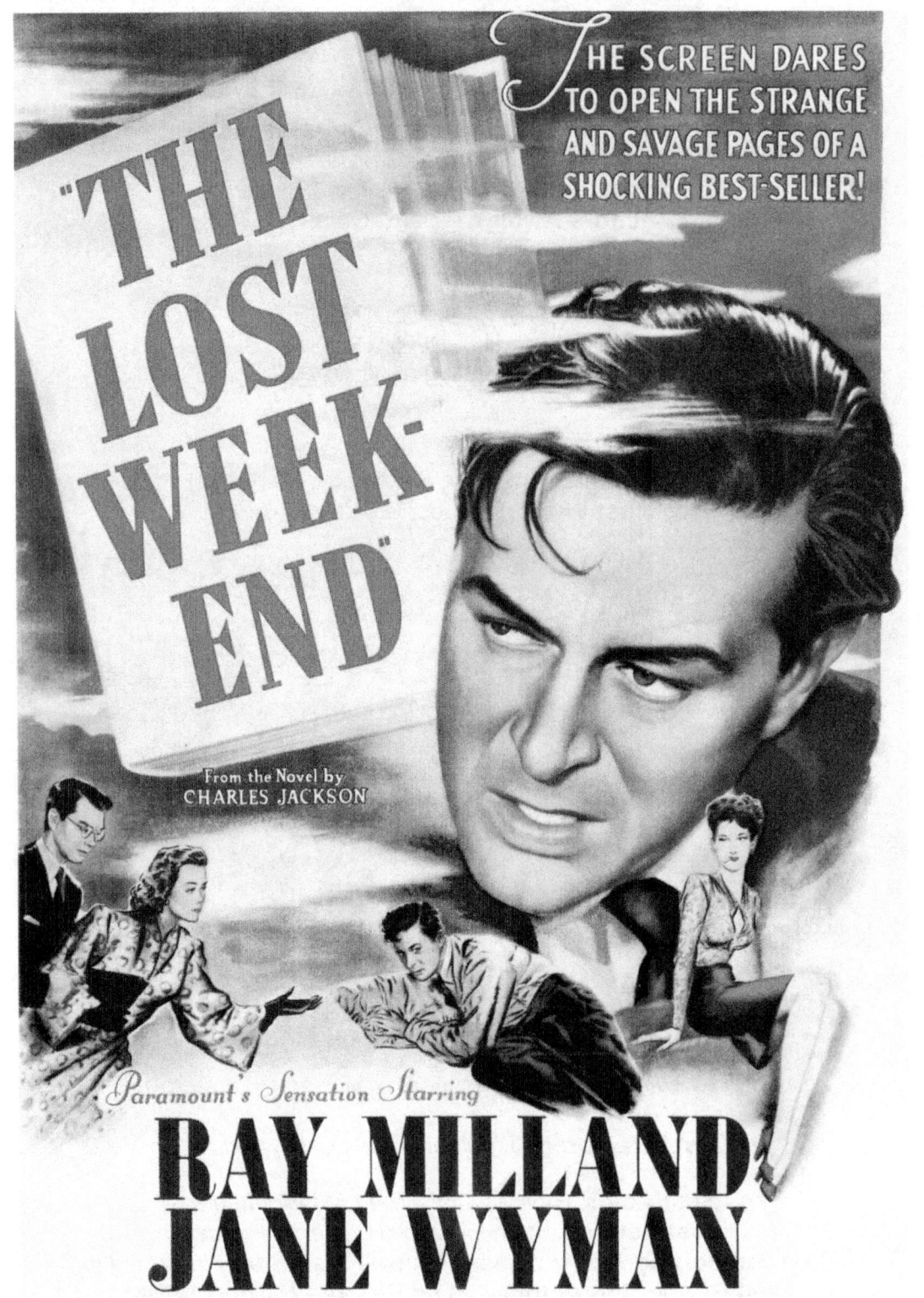

Directed by: Billy Wilder - Runtime: 1h 41m

The desperate life of chronic alcoholic Don Birnam is followed through a four-day drinking bout.

Starring

Ray Milland
b. 3rd January 1907
d. 10th March 1986
Character:
Don Birnam

Jane Wyman
b. 5th January 1917
d. 10th September 2007
Character:
Helen St. James

Phillip Terry
b. 7th March 1909
d. 23rd February 1993
Character:
Wick Birnam

Trivia

Interesting Facts

Ray Milland checked himself into Bellevue Hospital, New York, with the help of resident doctors in order to experience the horror of a drunk ward. Milland was given an iron bed and locked inside the "booze tank". That night, a new arrival came into the ward screaming, an entrance that immersed the whole ward in hysteria. With the ward falling into bedlam, a robed and barefoot Milland escaped while the door was ajar and slipped out onto 34th Street where he tried to hail a cab. When a suspicious cop spotted him Milland tried to explain but the cop didn't believe him, especially after he noticed the Bellevue insignia on his robe. The actor was dragged back to Bellevue where it took him half an hour to explain his situation to the authorities before he was finally released.

The Lost Weekend was the first film to feature a theremin on the soundtrack (a musical instrument that produces a strange "wailing" sound that was later used in many 1950s science-fiction films). Miklós Rózsa used it in composing the score for the nightmare sequences.

The original novel the film is based on has the character referring to a homosexual affair, but the script was changed so that the main character was suffering from writer's block.

Ray Milland didn't give an acceptance speech at the Academy Awards when he picked up his Best Actor Oscar. He merely acknowledged the crowd's applause and then left the podium without saying anything.

Quotes

Don Birnam: Just give me another drink.
Nat: Mr. Birnam, this is the morning?
Don Birnam: That's when you need it most - in the morning. Haven't you learned that yet? At night this stuff's a drink. In the morning, it's medicine.

The Bells of St. Mary's

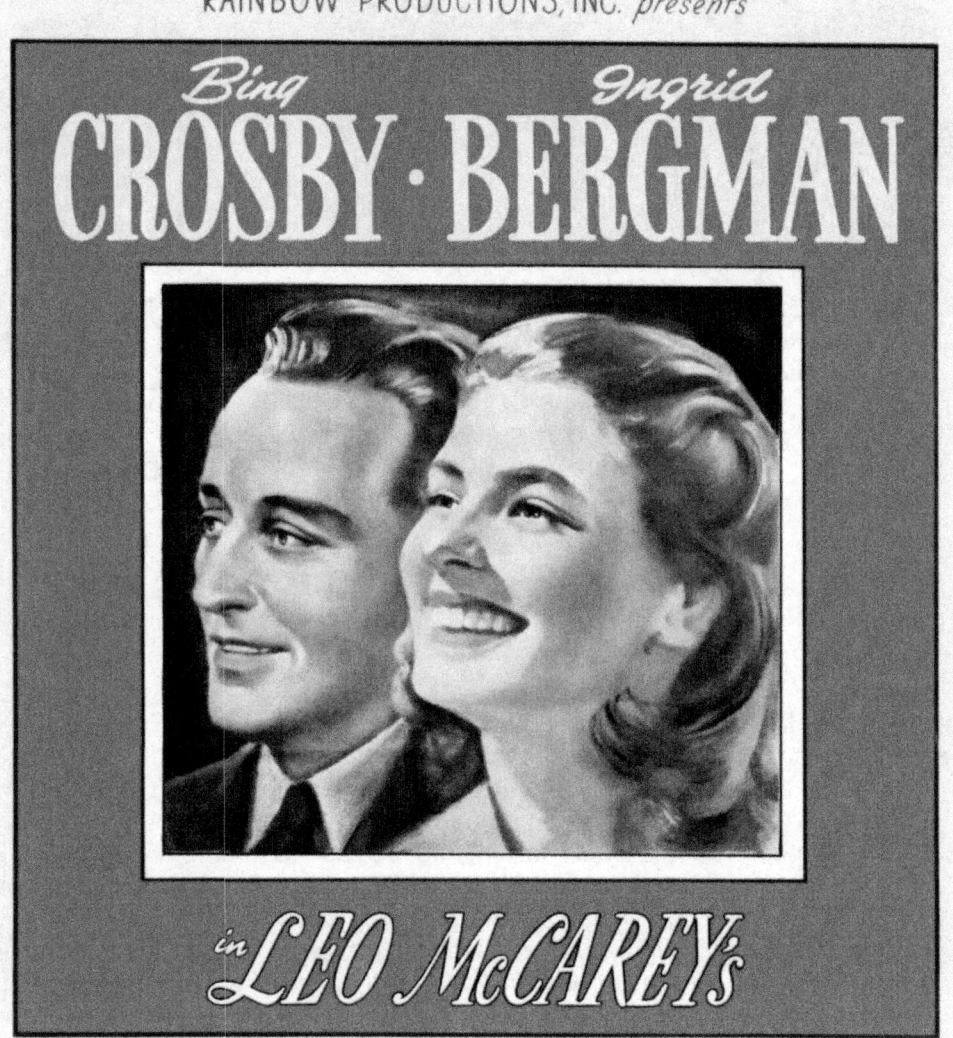

Directed by: Leo McCarey - Runtime: 2h 6m

At a big city Catholic school, Father O'Malley and Sister Benedict indulge in friendly rivalry, and succeed in extending the school through the gift of a building.

Starring

Bing Crosby
b. 3rd May 1903
d. 14th October 1977
Character:
Father Chuck O'Malley

Ingrid Bergman
b. 29th August 1915
d. 29th August 1982
Character:
Sister Mary Benedict

Henry Travers
b. 5th March 1874
d. 18th October 1965
Character:
Horace P. Bogardus

Trivia

Goof | Sister Mary Benedict buys a training manual entitled "The Art of Boxing" by Gene Tunney. In reality, Tunney, a legendary prize-fighter, never wrote such a book, although he did write two autobiographies.

Interesting Facts | The production was overseen by a Catholic priest who served as an advisor during the shooting. While the final farewell sequence was being filmed, Bing Crosby and Ingrid Bergman decided to play a prank on him. They asked director Leo McCarey to allow one more take, and, as "Father O'Malley" and "Sister Benedict" said their last goodbyes, they embraced in a passionate kiss, while the off-screen priest / advisor jumped up roaring in protest.

Leo McCarey was inspired to write the original story in tribute to his own aunt and childhood counsellor Sister Mary Benedict, one of the sisters who helped to build the Immaculate Heart Convent in Los Angeles, California.

Bing Crosby's performance as Father O'Malley earned him an Oscar nomination for Best Actor, the first time a person had received a nomination for playing the same character in two different films (he had been nominated, and won, for Going My Way (1944) the previous year).

Quotes | *Sister Mary Benedict:* You don't become a nun to run away from life Patsy. It's not because you've lost something. It's because you've found something.

Father Chuck O'Malley: [singing] Every time you're near a rose, aren't you glad you've got a nose?

MILDRED PIERCE

Directed by: Michael Curtiz - Runtime: 1h 51m

A hard-working mother inches towards disaster as she divorces her husband and starts a successful restaurant business to support her spoiled daughter.

Starring

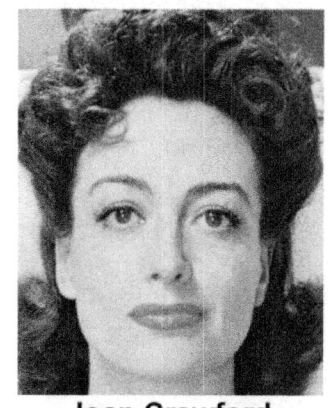

Joan Crawford
b. 23rd March 1904
d. 10th May 1977
Character:
Mildred Pierce Beragon

Jack Carson
b. 27th October 1910
d. 2nd January 1963
Character:
Wally Fay

Zachary Scott
b. 21st February 1914
d. 3rd October 1965
Character:
Monte Beragon

Trivia

Goof | Mildred's house on Corvallis Street in Glendale is shown as a one-story Spanish-style bungalow, however, the interior has a staircase leading to the bedrooms.

Interesting Facts | Director Michael Curtiz was initially less than keen at working with Joan Crawford but was soon won over by her dedication and hard work.

Mirroring her role in Mildred Pierce, Joan Crawford also supported herself as a waitress and saleswoman before she achieved success as an actress.

Monte's beach house, used in the key opening scene and several others, was owned by the film's director, Michael Curtiz. It was built in 1929 and stood on Latigo Shore Drive in Malibu. It collapsed into the ocean after a week of heavy storms in January 1983.

After seeing the film, author James M. Cain sent Joan Crawford a signed first edition of the original novel. The inscription read: "To Joan Crawford, who brought Mildred Pierce to life just as I had always hoped she would be, and who has my lifelong gratitude".

Quotes | *Mildred Pierce:* That Ted Forrester's nice-looking, isn't he? Veda likes him.
Monte Beragon: Who wouldn't? He has a million dollars.

Ida Corwin: [to Wally about his lustful looks in her direction] Leave something on me. I might catch cold.

SPELLBOUND

Directed by: Alfred Hitchcock - Runtime: 1h 51m

A psychiatrist protects the identity of an amnesia patient accused of murder while attempting to recover his memory.

Starring

Ingrid Bergman
b. 29th August 1915
d. 29th August 1982
Character:
Dr. Constance Petersen

Gregory Peck
b. 5th April 1916
d. 12th June 2003
Character:
John Ballantyne

Michael Chekhov
b. 16th August 1891
d. 30th September 1955
Character:
Dr. Alexander Brulov

Trivia

Goof | The burn on John Ballantyne's hand is only visible when Dr. Petersen notices it. It disappears in every other scene where his hand is visible.

Interesting Facts | Director Alfred Hitchcock was a big admirer of Salvador Dalí's work and brought him in to capture the vividness of dreams in the film's dream sequence. Producer David O. Selznick was opposed to using Dalí from an expense point of view, until he realised the marketing mileage that could be gained hiring him.

The snow falling on John Ballantyne and Dr. Petersen during the skiing scene is actually cornflakes.

Gregory Peck implied in a 1987 interview with People Magazine that he had an affair with Ingrid Bergman during the making of Spellbound.

Alfred Hitchcock referred to this film as "just another manhunt wrapped up in pseudo-psychoanalysis".

Quotes | *Constance Petersen:* All analysts have to be psychoanalysed by other analysts before they start practicing.
John Ballantyne: Ahhh, that's to make sure that they're not too crazy.

Dr. Alex Brulov: What is there for you to see? We both know that the mind of a woman in love is operating on the lowest level of the intellect!

ANCHORS AWEIGH

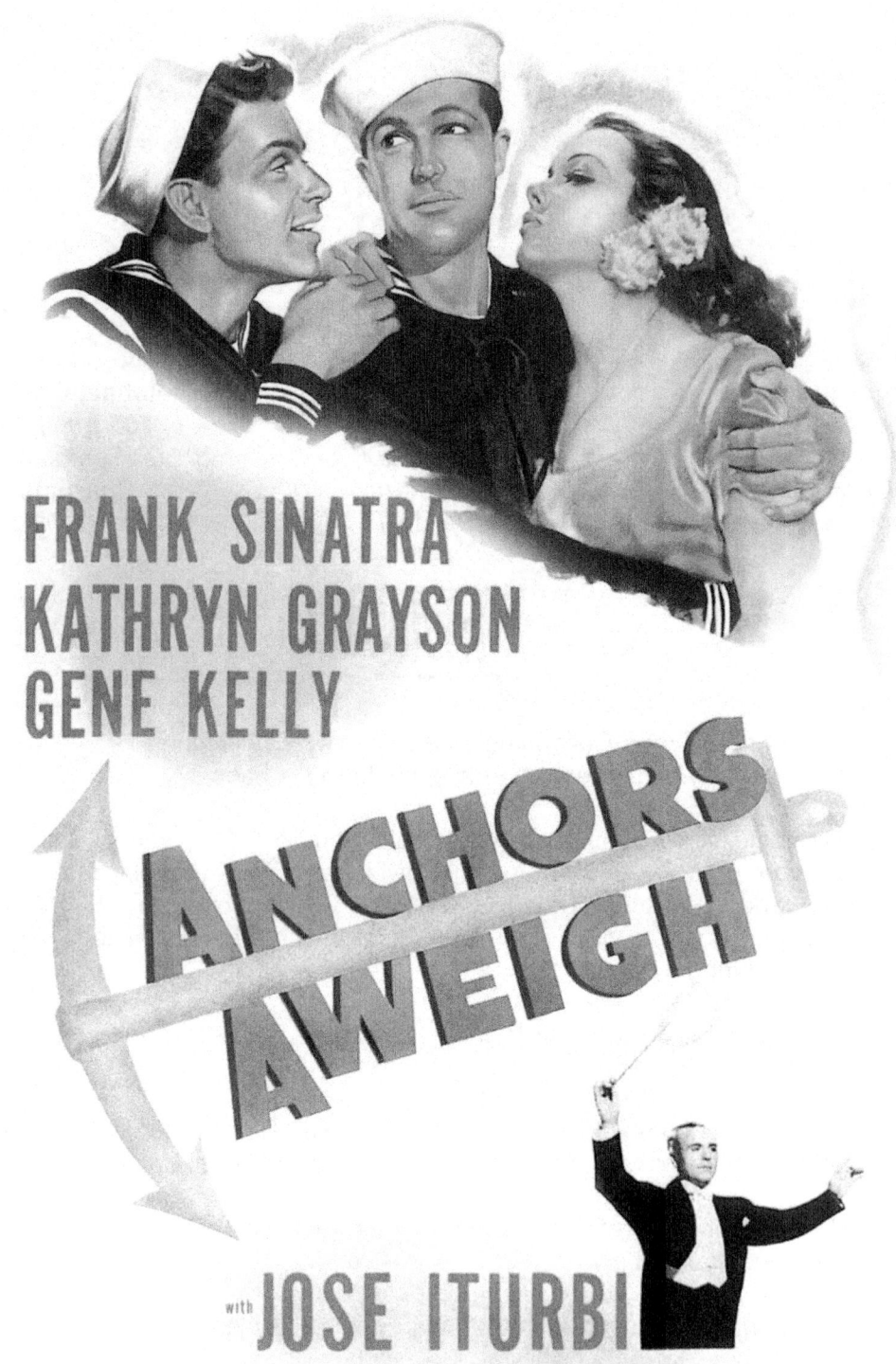

Directed by: George Sidney / Joseph Barbera / William Hanna - Runtime: 2h 20m

Joe and Clarence, two navy sailors who have a few days leave in Hollywood, try to help a movie extra become a singing star.

Starring

Frank Sinatra
b. 12th December 1915
d. 14th May 1998
Character:
Clarence Doolittle

Kathryn Grayson
b. 9th February 1922
d. 17th February 2010
Character:
Susan Abbott

Gene Kelly
b. 23rd August 1912
d. 2nd February 1996
Character:
Joseph Brady

Trivia

Goof | When Clarence is singing to the waitress in the restaurant there is a picture of Susita in the background. When seen at a distance her head is tilted to the left, but in a closeup her head is vertical.

Interesting Facts | When the dance sequence with Gene Kelly and cartoon character Jerry Mouse was screened for MGM executives, someone noticed that although Gene Kelly's reflection shone on the floor during his dancing, Jerry's did not. This required animators William Hanna and Joseph Barbera, and their team, to go back and draw Jerry's reflection on the floor as he was dancing. Additional money had to be allocated to cover the cost of the 10,000 new drawings needed.

Anchors Aweigh was Gene Kelly's first opportunity to choreograph an entire film himself.

It took Frank Sinatra eight weeks to learn the dance routine for the berthing area scene. Ultimately, it took 72 takes to get the right footage, though this was probably more due to Gene Kelly's meticulous need for perfection rather than Sinatra's inexperience as a dancer. Sinatra later said that he could have made an entire film in eight weeks.

Gene Kelly and Frank Sinatra collaborated on two other films after Anchors Aweigh, Take Me Out to the Ball Game (1949) and On the Town (1949).

Quotes | *Clarence Doolittle:* What makes the sunset? What makes the moon rise? Is it my love for you?

Jerry Mouse: Look at me, I'm dancing.

SPORTING WINNERS

Football

Between 1939 and 1946 normal competitive football was suspended in England and Scotland as many players had signed up to fight in the war. As a result, many teams were depleted and fielded guest players instead.

England: The 1944-1945 season was the sixth season of special wartime football in England. The Football League and FA Cup were suspended and replaced with regional competitions. Appearances in these tournaments did not count in players' official records.

Competition	Winner
League South	Tottenham Hotspur
League West	Cardiff City
League North	Huddersfield Town (1st Championship)
	Derby County (2nd Championship)
League North Cup	Derby County
Football League War Cup	Bolton Wanderers (Northern Section)
	Chelsea (Southern Section)
	Bolton beat Chelsea 2-1 in a playoff

Scotland: The 1944-1945 season was the sixth season of special wartime football in Scotland. The Scottish Football League and Scottish Cup were suspended and replaced with regional competitions. Appearances in these tournaments did not count in players' official records.

Competition	Winner
Southern League	Rangers
North-Eastern League (Autumn)	Dundee
North-Eastern League (Spring)	Aberdeen
Glasgow Cup	Rangers
Southern League Cup	Rangers
Summer Cup	Partick Thistle
Victory In Europe Cup	Celtic
Renfrewshire Cup	Morton
North-Eastern League Cup (Autumn)	Aberdeen
North-Eastern League Cup (Spring)	Aberdeen
East of Scotland Shield	Hibernian
Forfarshire Cup	Dundee

Unofficial International Matches

Date	Team	Score	Team	Date	Team	Score	Team
6th Jan	Belgium	2-3	Scotland	21st July	Switzerland	3-1	England
7th Jan	Flanders	6-4	Scotland	21st July	Switzerland B	0-3	England
3rd Feb	England	3-2	Scotland	15th Sep	Ireland	0-1	England
14th Apr	Scotland	1-6	England	20th Oct	England	0-1	Wales
5th May	Wales	2-3	England	10th Nov	Scotland	2-0	Wales
26th May	England	2-2	France				

Rugby - Home Nations

The 1945 Home Nations Championship series was not contested due to the war. International rugby was put on hold and would not resume again until 1947, when the Home Nations would become the Five Nations with the addition of France to the line-up.

Horse Racing

Grand National: Although the Grand National was run as normal in 1940 and most other major horse races around the world were able to be held throughout the war, the commandeering of Aintree for defence use in 1941 meant the Grand National could not be held between 1941 and 1945.

The Derby Stakes is Britain's richest horse race and the most prestigious of the country's five Classics. First run in 1780 this Group 1 flat horse race is open to three year old thoroughbred colts and fillies. Although the race usually takes place at Epsom Downs in Surrey, during both World Wars the venue was changed and the Derby was held at Newmarket - these races are known as the "New Derby". *Note: Epsom Downs racecourse was used for an anti-aircraft battery throughout World War II.*

Dante Derby 1945
Churchill 'J' Series

Winner	Jockey	Trainer	Owner	Prize Money
Dante	Billy Nevett	Matt Peacock	Sir Eric Ohlson	£8,339

Tennis - Wimbledon

The 1945 Wimbledon Championships was another sporting event cancelled due to World War II. Hosted since 1877 by the All England Lawn Tennis and Croquet Club, the competition did not resume again until 1946.

Cricket

With the end of the war in Europe in early May 1945, it was possible to organise eleven first-class cricket matches. These were the first to be played in England since 1939, though none were part of any official competition.

Victory Tests:
England 2-2 Australian Services

The Victory Tests were a series of cricket matches played in England between 19th May and 22nd August 1945, less than two weeks after the end of the war in Europe. Contested by a combined Australian Services XI and an English national side, they were never actually given Test match status by the participating Boards of Control because the Australian Cricket Board feared their side was not strong enough to compete with a near Test strength England. In all 367,000 spectators watched the teams play five three day matches at Lord's, Bramall Lane and Old Trafford.

Game	Ground	Result
1	Lord's, London	Australian Services won by 6 wickets
2	Bramall Lane, Sheffield	England won by 41 runs
3	Lord's, London	Australian Services won by 4 wickets
4	Lord's, London	Match drawn
5	Old Trafford, Manchester	England won by 6 wickets

Golf - Open Championship

The Open Championship was not held in 1945 due to the war and would not be contested again until 1946.

World Snooker Championship

The World Snooker Championship was cancelled because of the war and would not be held again until 1946.

The Cost of Living

Comparison Chart

	1945	1945 (+ Inflation)	2023	% Change
3 Bedroom House	£1,750	£92,202	£283,615	+207.6%
Weekly Income	£3.12s.1d	£189.89	£682	+259.2%
Pint Of Beer	9d	£1.98	£4.58	+131.3%
Cheese (lb)	1s.9d	£4.61	£3.40	-26.2%
Bacon (lb)	1s.11d	£5.05	£4.08	-19.2%
The Beano	2d	44p	£3.25	+638.6%

(1945-2023 cumulative rate of inflation: 5,168.68%)

Shopping

Loaf of Bread (4lb)	8d
Quaker Malted Wheat Flakes (pkt.)	5½d
Welgar Shredded Wheat	8d
Weetabix (small)	7½d
Symington's Soups (small packet)	2d
Fry's Cocoa Drink (¼lb)	5d
Bovril (1oz bottle)	7½d
Marmite (16oz jar)	4s.8d
Rowntree's Fine Chocolate	4d
Rowntree's Fruit Gums	2d
Eve Shampoo	3d
Milton Under Arm Rinse	8d
Personality Turtle Oil Soap	1s.10d
Palmolive Soap (tablet)	4d
Sunlight Soap (tablet)	3½d
Tek Toothbrush (nylon)	1s.10d
Gibbs Dentifrice	7½d
Pepsodent Toothpaste	1s.3d
Lever's Easy Shaving Stick	7½d
Gillette Steel Shaving Blade	2d
Tangee Lipstick (medium)	2s.11d
Atkinsons Skin Deep Beauty Cream	5s.10d
Icilma Foundation Cream (jar)	10½d
Zubes (tin)	8d
Rennies (25)	7d
Phensic Flu Tablets	1s.4d
Potter's Asthma Cure	2s.2d
Seven Seas Cod Liver Oil (standard)	1s.6d
Crooke's Halibut Oil (100 capsules)	8s.6d
Eno's Fruit Salt (bottle)	2s
Oxydol Washing Soap	7d
Vim (canister)	7d
Dettol	1s.5d
Sanitas Antiseptic	1s.1½d

Weetabix
MORE than a Breakfast Food

SMALL SIZE 2 POINTS 7½D.   LARGE SIZE 4 POINTS 1/1D.

Weetabix Ltd., Burton Latimer, Northants   WX 5

Other Items

Austin 16 HP Saloon	£569
Gallon Of Petrol	1s.11d
Harvey Nichols Jumper Suit	£10.9s
C&A Flower Print Frock	£2.3s.11d
Dewar's White Label Whisky	£1.5s.9d
Booth's Dry Gin	£1.5s.3d
Maldano Cocktails	14s.6d
Three Threes Cigarettes (20)	2s.4d
De Reszke Minors Cigarettes (20)	1s.9d
Craven Plain Cigarettes (10)	1s.2d
Woman's Weekly Magazine	3d
Daily Express Newspaper	1d
Daily Mirror Newspaper	1d

Money Conversion Table

Pounds / Shillings / Pence 'Old Money'		Decimal Value	Value 2023 (Rounded)
Farthing	¼d	0.1p	5p
Half Penny	½d	0.21p	11p
Penny	1d	0.42p	22p
Threepence	3d	1.25p	66p
Sixpence	6d	2.5p	£1.32
Shilling	1s	5p	£2.63
Florin	2s	10p	£5.27
Half Crown	2s.6d	12.5p	£6.59
Crown	5s	25p	£13.17
Ten Shillings	10s	50p	£26.34
Pound	20s	£1	£52.69
Guinea	21s	£1.05	£55.32
Five Pounds	£5	£5	£263.43
Ten Pounds	£10	£10	£526.87

IT is the £1 Certificate, worth 23/- after 10 years, and although you may already hold your full quota of 500 Certificates issued at any price under £1, you can acquire in addition a maximum of 250 of these £1 Certificates, giving you a profit in 10 years of £37 10s. 0d. on which there is no tax to pay! They can be bought for cash or in exchange for Savings Stamps through your Savings Group or your bank, or at any Post Office, Trustee Savings Bank, or Savings Centre.

£1 NATIONAL SAVINGS Certificates

Issued by the National Savings Committee

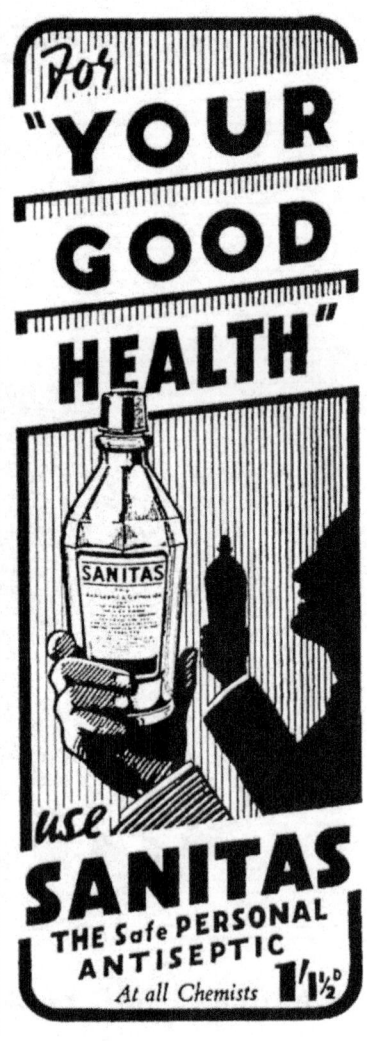

April Showers bring May Flowers

PALMOLIVE BRINGS THAT SCHOOLGIRL COMPLEXION

PALMOLIVE
4d. Including Tax

Expert Guidance

No more expert guidance can be offered than the selection of "Black & White" as a tonic. This skilfully blended fine old Scotch Whisky relieves the strain and stress of the present time.

It's the Scotch!

"BLACK & WHITE"

Printed in Great Britain
by Amazon